THE
BIRTH
OF AN AMERICAN
MEDIUM

A MEMOIR

JAMES DEARY

Copyright © 2023 by James Deary.

All rights reserved. Published in the United States by Citrine Publishing, LLC, State College, Pennsylvania.

Thank you for complying with international copyright laws by not scanning, reproducing, or distributing any part of this book in any form without permission, except in the case of brief quotations included in articles and reviews. For information, address Permissions@CitrinePublishing.com.

This is a work of nonfiction. Nonetheless, some names, identifying details, and personal characteristics of the individuals involved have been changed. The author of this book does not dispense medical advice or prescribe the use of any technique as a form of treatment for physical, emotional, or medical problems without the advice of a physician, either directly or indirectly. The intent of the author is only to offer information of a general nature to help you in your quest for well-being. In the event you use any of the information in the book for yourself, which is your constitutional right, the author and publisher assume no responsibility for your actions.

Library of Congress Cataloging-in-Publication Data

Deary, James

The Birth of an American Medium: A Memoir

p. cm.

Paperback ISBN: 978-1-954569-08-9

Ebook ISBN: 978-1-954569-98-0

Library of Congress Control Number: 2023911421

First Trade Paperback Edition, July 2023

CITRINE PUBLISHING

State College, Pennsylvania, U.S.A.

www.CitrinePublishing.com

For information about special discounts for group purchases, please call +1-828-585-7030 or email Sales@CitrinePublishing.com.

For Sallie

You are always understanding.

Cover Photo: James Deary at age five, September 1950

Praise for *The Birth of an American Medium*

"James Deary shares an interesting and captivating story as he takes you with him on an exciting journey through his life. The vulnerability he shares as he grapples with the realization, and ultimately, his acceptance of his mediumship and psychic abilities, will bring comfort to others on the same journey. A well-written page-turner that will keep you wanting to read late into the night."

Leona Mc Nama-Gora, Spiritual Medium and Mentor

"A book that surprises in generous ways is rare. A writer who gracefully conveys the difficulty of self-revelation is to be celebrated. Deary's prophetic memoir unveiling himself as a psychic can serve as a relief manual for all hidden selves. Who one is and what one is capable of takes bravery. This book is a pilgrimage. Lucid, exciting, sometimes weird and amazing, always true and honorable, it never ceases to be an adventure story. Deary's perception captures the human spirit—both alive and dead."

Julie Gilbert, Pulitzer Prize nominated author

"A joy to read! You will be captivated by the unique experiences that James relates so vividly. From his international work experience and his spiritual encounters to the writing of this book...courage is the emotion that fills the heart. I could not put this book down! This is a must read for anyone who is being tapped on the shoulder by Spirit."

Michelle Robin, Spiritual Medium

Praise for *The Birth of an American Medium*

"Growing up with a father in the FBI, a famous uncle, and a mother who would sometimes see people 'who weren't there,' James had a childhood that was anything but ordinary. Tracing his journey through various places in the world, this book unfurls the story of a man whose psychic abilities were something he wished to have no part of...until decades later, when he realized he couldn't deny them any longer. Carefully chosen, thoughtfully written, amazing stories abound in this book that ultimately result in one man's decision to embrace Spirit, every day of his life."

Jaime Cox, Editor

"In this fascinating memoir, evidential psychic medium James Deary describes his many surprising, unexplainable, and sometimes frightening otherworldly experiences which started in his childhood. James suppressed and denied those events during his pathway to destiny. He takes the reader inside his mind as he encounters one mystical event after another during his evolution from a closeted, self-doubting clairvoyant to a practicing psychic medium. After discovering the healing benefits of mediumship, he surrendered to full acceptance of his God-given gift, and honed his mediumship abilities through intensive training. James currently renders his service to those who suffer from grief. His message to readers is that we survive beyond death, mediumship is spiritual in nature, and prayer is important."

Emily Rodavich, Author of *Mystical Interludes* and Founder of the Mystical Interludes Discussion Group

Contents

Prologue IX
Preface XIII

My Family 17
My First Experience with Death: The Swimming Pool 21
My First Psychic Experience 29
Little Indian Boy 33
Store-Front Psychic 37
Three Priests 41
Two Faces of Evil 47
Medium in the Georgia Mountains 53
Haunted by the Past 61
Voices of War 65
Dachau Memory 71
I Saw the Dead Soldier 75
The Proof Is in Your Palm 77
Spooky London 81
The Boston Tea Room Psychic 85
The Harvard Astrologer 89
The Psychic Psychologist 93
Pizza Synchronicity 95
Female House Spirit 103

Spirit Guide Visitation	107
Religious Visions	111
A Second Dream Visitation	115
Uninvited Dinner Guests	119
The Beach House Haunting	121
The Ghost Speaks	129
Even in Death, We Do Not Part	135
Spirit in the Boardroom	139
Dr. Edgeworth: Another Spirit Guide	143
Who Can Help Me?	147
Angel in the Classroom	151
Belief and Confidence	157
A Second Near-Death Experience	161
Holy Cannoli, I Can Hear	167
Spirits in the Storm	173
Spirits of Sedona	179
An Irish Story	189
Double Apparition	195
A Call from Heaven	199
Epilogue	203
Acknowledgments	205

Prologue

2008

At 7:00 a.m., my psychic energy increased. The spirit of a male drew close. My mind and body entered a state of receptivity as I shifted my awareness, and in an instant, a "spirit-energy" entered my clairvoyant awareness. Visions and psychic information washed over me, and I took notes and drew pictures of everything. Waves of energy showered over me.

Within my altered state of consciousness, I was looking down at a shiny, white, bald head. A figure was lying on its back, on something that brought it level to my waist. I was behind its head, looking down toward the top of its chest. It appeared to be on a raised bed. As my teacher had suggested, with my mind, I asked the spirit energy to step back and wait until after I dialed the sitter. Often, I receive precognitive information from Spirit prior to the arrival of a client.

I finished making notes at 8:00 a.m. and dialed the number I had received from a psychic medium friend in Boston. I had an arrangement with a few psychics who would send me the first name and phone number of clients who couldn't afford the standard consulting fee. My readings were always complimentary for grief-stricken individuals.

On the third ring, a woman answered. Still in a heightened state of awareness, I introduced myself and explained that though I usually connect with a spirit, it may not be of the deceased person she expected to hear from. I asked her not to reveal anything about herself or her family members—"yes" or "no" to any of my questions would be sufficient. I told her that I wanted to communicate enough specific information to her that she was convinced beyond a doubt that I had connected with at least one of her deceased loved ones. I shared that the reason I do this work is to prove to the client that there is continuity of life after death. I then apologized to her for having had to reschedule her reading—twice. As she thanked me for calling her, I put the phone on speaker, closed my eyes, and began.

"I'm looking down at a white bald head. It's very shiny. The person is lying on their back. I'm standing behind them. They are at my waist level as if they were lying on a bed. Do you understand any of this?"

"No. I don't know what any of that means," she replied.

Oh no, I thought to myself with a twinge of disappointment. But it was not the first time I had received a negative response from a client, so I pushed on.

"Now I'm standing in front of a log cabin with three steps leading up to a front porch. There's green grass in front of it. I also see pine trees in the front yard. About fifty yards from the front of the cabin is a lake. Do you understand this place?" I asked.

"Yes," she whispered in surprise. Feeling some relief, I continued.

"There's a man standing in front of the cabin. He's short with short dark hair. Forgive me for sounding impolite, but he has an Elmer Fudd appearance. He wants you to know that he has fond memories of this location. He says he spent a lot of time here with you and that he enjoyed fishing here on the lake. He wants you to know how sorry he is. Does this make any sense to you?"

"Yes," the woman answered angrily.

Her anger startled me. Normally clients were happy when I was able to connect with a spirit they could identify.

"I didn't want him to communicate with me today." Her reply unsettled me, but I continued anyway.

"Now I see another man. He's standing in front of the same cabin at the lake. The first man is no longer there. This man is much taller. He walks with his body bent forward. He looks a little like President Abraham Lincoln. Can you understand any of this?" I asked.

"Yes, everything you said makes a lot of sense. The first man you described was my ex-husband. I had a relationship with the second man after my husband left me. At different times, each of those men lived with me in the log cabin on the lake you described. I was very happy that the second man came through. He's the one I wanted to hear from today. I really didn't want to hear from my ex-husband. He passed away shortly after he left me. I loved the second man very much," she said.

"I feel your husband died of cancer," I continued.

"That's right. He had cancer," the woman said.

"The second man, who looked like Abe Lincoln, had a drinking problem," I said.

"Yes," she replied with sadness in her voice.

"But he's not telling me how he passed," I said.

I knew from experience that when a spirit was reluctant to tell me, it was often because they had, in some way, been responsible for their passing. I didn't reveal this to the woman.

Suddenly, just when I thought the reading was coming to an end—"The spirit of a woman is coming forward. She is tall and has long blonde hair. Her skin is very white and she's waving her arms as if to get my attention. They are very long and graceful," I said.

The woman was silent. I gave her time to consider the information I had shared.

"My relationship with the second man lasted only a few years. Yes, he did look a little like Abe Lincoln. And, yes, he did have a terrible time with alcohol."

"I feel that he was a very gentle soul. His energy feels very different from that of your ex-husband," I said.

"Yes. Yes, he was. The girl you described—the tall blonde with long arms—she was his girlfriend after his drinking came between us," she said.

"She's telling me that she too passed from cancer. She's pointing to her abdomen."

"Yes. She died from stomach cancer." There was a long pause. "The man who looked like Abe Lincoln committed suicide. It happened right after the blonde woman died from stomach cancer," she said softly.

"I'm so sorry for all your loss," I offered. I paused. "Before we finish today, I want to ask you about the white, shiny, bald head that I mentioned earlier in the reading. Neither your husband nor your boyfriend were bald. Do you have any idea why this vision has stayed in my mind for the past three days?"

Suddenly, the woman's laughter poured into my room through the speaker, instantly creating a more positive and upbeat energy.

"I'm a student of massage therapy and I practice massage every day on a shiny, white, rubber dummy! And, yes, I stand behind its head during my practice sessions," she said, clearly smiling. I was glad for the aha moment.

"Thank you for allowing me to channel your loved ones today. Please know that—even now—your ex-husband expresses hope that you're able to release the anger you hold around his memory. He says he remembers the good times at the cabin and wishes you would as well," I said. Then, after a moment, "Also, I apologize for rescheduling your appointment, twice. I have never done that to a client before."

There was another pause.

"You know what? Today is his birthday! Today is my ex-husband's birthday!" she shouted.

"I don't believe in coincidence. I believe that your ex-husband has given you a gift from the other side. I've never postponed a reading twice. I think this was his way of having us wait until his birthday," I said. At this point in my mediumship development, I had never had *three* spirits come through. But I kept that to myself.

A week later, I received an email from her with four photos attached: one of her ex-husband, who looked a bit like Lincoln, another of her boyfriend, who absolutely had an Elmer Fudd appearance, a tall blonde woman with exceptionally long arms, and finally, a picture of the shiny, white, bald-headed dummy that she used to practice her massage techniques.

Preface

I was most likely born a psychic medium. From early childhood, I could see the spirit of dead people. Much later in life, I was able to receive messages from them, giving evidence to their family and friends that they were still here with us. I also "knew" things about the living, things I was later able to confirm to be true. This ability may sound unique and interesting, but it is often disturbing and unnerving. As a youngster, I didn't think I was any different from anyone else. I thought my knowing ability was just part of being a human. My earliest memory of these abilities traces back to when I saw my first apparition at age eight—I will describe that later.

As a young child, Mom kept me close and often took me with her whenever she had an errand to run. I had a lot of experience with supermarkets and women's clothing stores...two locations I resist visiting today. I suppose she was giving our grandmother a break for awhile—one less kid in the house. But I later learned that there were three additional reasons why Mom had wanted me nearby. She had lost her first male child to a blood incompatibility problem that led to a miscarriage. Then, she almost lost her second child. When I was two, I came very close to drowning. (I was blue when my aunt dragged me out of a swimming pool.) Maybe, more importantly, the real reason why my mother kept me close was because we were both clairvoyant. We had an ability to see the spirits of those who had passed over—we both saw ghosts!

Mom would rarely mention anything when she saw a spirit. It was not the kind of information that was talked about back in those days. The only time you would hear the word "ghost" was when the cartoon, *Casper the Friendly Ghost,* was on TV. Everybody believed there was no such thing as ghosts. The one occasion that Mom announced to the family that she had seen a spirit led to bursts of laughter. The look on everyone's faces firmly convinced me that no one believed it was possible to see dead people. They thought you were crazy if you thought you could. I didn't want to be thought of that way, so I kept my mouth shut... for a very long time. The fear of being labeled as crazy haunted me. I suppose to some extent, it still does. I definitely avoided going public with anything that happened to me that was out of the ordinary or other-worldly. I avoided anything and everything related to my psychic abilities. I was "in the closet," leading two lives.

As I grew up and began to experience more and more psychic phenomenon, I couldn't understand why stuff was happening only to me. I couldn't explain it to myself, so I certainly wasn't eager to attempt to explain it to someone else—plus there wasn't anyone else *to* discuss it with. Avoidance was a necessity for a young boy growing up in the fifties and sixties. Kids want to fit in with their friends, family, and society in general. For that matter, so do adults. I didn't want to be different. No one does.

Teachers, parish priests, parents, and even President Kennedy told us young people to "get a good education then go out and become a productive member of society." Psychic Medium was not on the list of career options in the sixties. Had my abilities been part of the social discourse as they are today, I very well may have embraced them much earlier in life.

What I *did* embrace was the call to become a productive member of society. Since 1969, I've worked in professional settings in Europe and the United States. I was educated at the doctoral level, served as a secondary school headmaster in Europe, and co-founded a successful health care organization in New York City in 1984 that meets the needs of thousands of the underserved in marginalized communities. I was certainly never in search of psychic or mediumship abilities.

This book is an account of the often strange and inexplicable experiences I've had since childhood. With these experiences came the great responsibility that comes with communicating with the other side. In the pages that follow, I will explain how my abilities would just "show up"—often at very inconvenient times: during my walks, in church, at work, and in hospitals. Spirits would even haphazardly show up at parties. (Mediums are well aware that none of our abilities come easily.)

Preface

While psychic experiences may sound interesting or even humorous at times, they can often be quite disturbing. Suddenly seeing a full-body apparition shakes the foundation of every belief we hold regarding science, religion, and reality itself.

Each and every—sometimes unbelievable—event described in the stories you are about to read, happened. I've tried to mainly include only those vignettes for which I was able to provide substantiation. I hope my words might provide some assistance and peace of mind to others who are on a similar path of spiritual understanding. What the reader does with their abilities is solely up to themselves and the spirit world, and no one else.

1

My Family

The best gift I've received in this life is that of always feeling loved as a child. I remember my grandmother and grandfather reminding me how lucky I was to have the parents I had. That didn't resonate with me as a young kid, but they were absolutely correct. Eight of us lived in my grandparents' modest house—a house more suited for half that number. We were close in more ways than one.

I'm not sure I realized it at the time, but my younger brothers, Kevin and Tom, and sister, Lenore, and I had things pretty good growing up. Mom and Nana were home every day taking care of the house, the cooking, their husbands, the four of us kids, and often, my cousins.

A golf course across the street served as a place to caddy to make money, play golf, and socialize with our friends. I have fond memories of our family eating quick dinners sometimes to leave time to play a few holes of golf before sunset. I was lucky without realizing *how* lucky. I was also the eldest. It's a birth position that comes with a lot of expectations, like setting an example for the younger children—the jury is still out on whether I met that one. My brothers and I were so close in age that we were often referred to as Irish triplets.

Then Lenore arrived—the daughter my mother had waited years for. Five years separated Lenore from me, four from Kevin, and three from Tom. Five years—that's a big age gap when you're a kid, and so, I didn't really get to know her till much later.

Dad, James Deary II, turned fifty when Lenore was thirteen. She grew up with a much different view of the family than her brothers had. She was the special granddaughter to Nana and Gramp Ed. She played golf very well but wanted independence from our male-dominated family. She and her best friend saved their babysitting money for years, and eventually purchased a palomino horse from a local farmer when she was fourteen. While her brothers and parents were out winning golf trophies, Lenore was winning blue ribbons for her riding and jumping skills. She continued winning blue ribbons for fifty years, right up until she passed away.

Dad was clearly the center of the family. He was first-generation Boston Irish. But Mom, Dad and I moved to Connecticut from Boston and right into my mother's parents' home. Dad knew that he'd be stationed in different cities during the next five years and didn't want his family moving from city to city around the country. Dad was very different than most of the other dads in our rural Connecticut town. He was highly educated, having been to college, graduate school, and law school. He also studied Greek and Latin at one point, in preparation for potentially entering into seminary school. Interestingly, instead, he had become a senior special agent in the Federal Bureau of Investigation and a good friend of its director, J. Edgar Hoover. During Hoover's forty-eight-year tenure, he was considered more powerful than the presidents.

Dad's experience included station work in Washington, D.C., Chicago, Philadelphia, Detroit, New York City, and Boston before being permanently stationed in the New Haven office. Throughout the years that Hoover served as director, the FBI controlled law enforcement in the United States. By the time Dad turned forty-seven and I had entered my teenage years, my father was one of the most powerful people in the state. Special Agent Deary was not only Dad, but also a symbol in my life. He exemplified hard work, education, law and order, respect for a higher being, and dedication to his wife, family, and country. I never knew exactly what he did each day after he left for work. He kept that information away from everyone in the house. One time in elementary school when the class was asked to describe their father's work, I was at a loss for words. Dad once told me that most Americans have no idea of the kind of people who are out there doing terrible things to each other and to our country. "The public doesn't need to know—that's my job," he'd say.

In many ways, Dad led two lives. He left the house every morning wearing a three-piece suit with a Colt revolver in his shoulder holster. He was the American version of James Bond and was licensed to kill. Mom was his counterpart: a beautiful blonde, ten years his junior. They were dedicated to each other—we kids were secondary. One day when Dad overheard me yelling at my mother for some adolescent reason, he got into my face and said, "Don't you ever talk to my wife like that!" That he didn't say "your mother," spoke volumes to me, even as a fourteen-year-old.

We were sent out to work as caddies at the local country club as soon as we were able to pick up a twenty-five-pound golf bag. When we complained, it fell on deaf ears—we would immediately be reminded about how our father had to sell eggs on the streets of Boston for a penny each when he was a kid. Nothing was handed to us, and we were taught the meaning of working hard for every dollar, and so we did: paper routes, lawn mowing, and snow shoveling was pretty much covered by us boys. Lenore cleaned the stables where she kept her palomino.

We were good kids, but we had our rebellious streaks now and then. We held the belief, not always conscious, that our mischief could never result in any real legal trouble for us because Dad wielded so much influence in the state. For example, the few times we'd been stopped for speeding, or caught throwing snowballs, or in minor car accidents, the police would let us go as soon as they heard our last name. They knew who our father was. Though we never flaunted this privilege, we knew Dad was our Get Out of Jail Free card.

My connection to power and influence was coupled with money, but not ours. Nana's brother Morton was a singer and movie star. He left home at sixteen, made millions in show business, and lived just a few houses away from us. So naturally, the townspeople thought that we too shared in his fortune. Quite the contrary. At a young age, I learned that most people cannot handle extreme wealth. Everyone on Earth thinks they can, but they can't...trust me on this one. Nevertheless, a famous millionaire relative on the street was fodder for local gossip.

I grew up within an extended family of four generations from Ireland, many of whom overcame great difficulties before and after their immigration to America. We lived our daily lives as Americans and not as an Irish family living in the USA. We celebrated St. Patrick's Day, but that was it. We also looked forward to special German meals that our Nana would prepare for Gramp Ed. We were truly Americans. Our nearby neighbors were a cultural mix of Greek, Jewish, Italian, and Polish.

Our neighborhood was a melting pot, as was America. The only fences in our community were those surrounding the farms so the animals wouldn't wander onto the golf course. Our neighbors had varying and differing beliefs, customs, and religions…everything was different, yet everyone got along. The environment was definitely not conducive to announcing that "the eldest Deary boy sees ghosts." If you don't count seeing ghosts, I lived what I thought was a fairly normal upbringing for that time.

Back then, it was easier to just live two lives.

2

My First Experience with Death: The Swimming Pool

"You know, you drowned in your uncle's swimming pool." It was the mid-eighties and my mother's extra-dry-martini voice had resonated above the chatter around the Thanksgiving Day table. Four generations of Irish Americans were cramped around it, patiently waiting to dig into the colorful dishes of food that decorated it. The whiskey-fueled appetites of my relatives were supercharged by various concoctions poured from bottles from the mahogany liquor cabinet. It was self-serve when it came to the booze. I have never heard anyone shout the words, "You've had enough!" at our dining table, and certainly not on a holiday.

I opened the back door to clear out the clouds of cigarette smoke that had accumulated on the ceiling. Thank God nobody smoked cigars. I refer back to times like those when I was asked the inevitable question posed to every kid, "How come you don't smoke?" Fact is, I never saw any difference between smoking cigarettes and standing behind the tailpipe of my grandfather's old Studebaker while it chugged blue exhaust. I still don't get it. By the way, I don't drink whiskey, either! Somehow, that part of the Irish gene missed me.

Eighteen adults were packed, sardine style, at a table made to seat a dozen. The younger children were banished downstairs to the basement to eat at card tables lined up against the cellar wall. I celebrated many holidays at those card tables as a youngster—"children should be seen but not heard," right?

My cousin Ann, who sat across the table from me that evening, had immediately noticed the expression of shock on my face after my mom's comment that had seemed to otherwise mostly fallen on deaf ears (and full mouths). Her expression led me to believe she knew something that I did not. I've had my share of startling moments in life, but that remark about my drowning definitely took the cake. I expected to hear an explanation from Ann as the hungry voices subsided a little.

Looking back, Norma's (my mother's) comment would have been adequate fodder for conversation at a normal dinner, but evidently, the topic was not suitable for discussion at Thanksgiving dinner on Country Club Lane. Perhaps no one had heard my mother, due to the loud chorus of drinking voices. But Norma, I knew, was a woman who was always heard and, more importantly, a woman who demanded that everyone listen.

The lack of response from the table meant one of two things. Either Ann and I were the only ones who had heard Norma, or everyone else already knew about the accident and just didn't care to discuss painful old news. Growing up in families we all learn behaviors that we're often not even aware of. This holiday, it dawned on me that my family never discussed emotionally charged topics that might render the family anything but "normal." You've heard about that imaginary perfect family that everyone yearns for, despite the fact that it doesn't exist. We all know better, but we still dream. If someone attempted a taboo discussion on a holiday or any other day, they were avoided like the plague. Everyone at the table suddenly became tone deaf.

This was one of those annual dinners that families plan around holiday time, usually out of a sense of duty. My two brothers, sister, and assorted cousins were young adults. However, our age didn't matter, we were still "the kids."

After all, Thanksgiving dinner is an American social experiment that attempts to keep a family connected from generation to generation. Who on Earth would have wanted to create friction and talk about the near-death drowning of a child? Everyone had come to have fun and visit with my grandmother. My mother's mother, or Nana as we called her, was the main attraction. Everyone loved her and held her in high esteem. She was not only the grandmother who lived with us, but also the woman who helped raise me (and my siblings, and my cousins) from childhood. Everyone in the house that day considered Bess their mother figure.

My family respected the unspoken rule that forbade the discussion of emotionally charged subject matter, especially during dinnertime. Some family rules, like Catholics must not eat meat on Fridays, didn't have to be spoken. Rules were understood and obeyed. This rule was in the air we breathed. No one dared break it. But Norma's comment that day chiseled a crack into that rule.

Maybe Norma's martini had encouraged her to break the rule today? I thought to myself.

After her comment fell on deaf ears, Mom announced she was headed to the kitchen to get her homemade black-bottom pie. She had discovered this unique dessert while on their honeymoon in Manhattan at the Waldorf Astoria in 1941. She proudly recalled how she walked into the Waldorf kitchen and asked the head chef for his recipe. Norma was never shy. With her charm and chutzpah, she coaxed his personal recipe out of him—that she was also gorgeous didn't hurt the negotiation. I suppose it's normal for a son to boast about his mother's beauty, but Norma really was beautiful. Shortly before she married Dad, a Hollywood movie producer offered to bring her to Los Angeles for screen tests after learning she could sing, dance, act, and memorize pages of dialogue. My uncle, Morton Downey, a Hollywood performer himself, stepped in and quickly put an end to that idea. He knew what could happen to a pretty teenage starlet alone in Hollywood. Morton and his wife were Hollywood actors. He reminded the family that Hollywood had a nickname, and it was SEX!

"Jimmy, it was my mother. It was Shirley who saved your life," my cousin Ann finally whispered across the table. I was speechless.

"Jimmy, Shirley rescued you from the swimming pool," Ann repeated more loudly.

Ann and I were very close growing up—neighbors who saw each other nearly every day. Our childhood joke was that we'd someday marry so we could continue to see each other daily.

I was dumbfounded that Ann had information that I did not. Have you ever been in a situation where everyone knew something that you didn't know, but should have? You feel a combination of isolated and stupid at the same time. The look on my face caught Ann by surprise. She didn't know that I didn't know what had happened to me.

"It happened at Uncle Morton's pool...when you were two years old. My mother pulled you up from the bottom of the pool. She said you were all blue," Ann revealed.

There were no words I could use to describe the reaction I felt when I heard about my near-death experience. I was too numb to ask questions. I figured that since the topic had apparently been a taboo subject for forty years, now was probably not the best time to resurrect it. My mind raced. Within a split second, I felt every possible emotion. My body temporarily short-circuited. Then my thoughts became angry. *How come nobody told me? Why was this kept from me?* Fear was my next emotion as I realized that had Aunt Shirley not been there that day...well, I didn't want to think about that outcome. I wanted to thank her, but at that table wasn't the time. I wasn't ready. *Did I die, or did I almost die?* I had no memory of that experience.

During the next few days, the enormity of that traumatic experience began to sink in. I remembered that my mother and her sister-in-law, Shirley, often took me across the street to Uncle Morton's swimming pool. I was too young to go into the water, so I'd play nearby on the lawn.

In 1947, Uncle Morton's— my grandmother's younger brother— was the only swimming pool in Wallingford, Connecticut. As a child, all I knew was that Morton and his wife were very rich and famous. Around the time I turned four or five, I began playing with Morton's children in the front yard of their home across the street from ours. I called it a mansion. Surprisingly, I never met Morton himself until I was eleven years old, at his mother's, my great-grandmother's, funeral. At that young age, I learned to associate fame and fortune with parents never being at home with their children. That's another one of those rules that got stuck in the back of my mind as a kid. "Watch out for fame and fortune if you want a happy family life," was the recording back then that still plays on in my head to this day.

My First Experience with Death: The Swimming Pool

My cousins were lucky if they saw their parents four times a year. Sorrow for my cousins was an emotion I remember quite well from childhood. I could actually *feel* their loneliness and unhappiness as I watched them acting out and could feel the anger attached to their behavior, even though I wasn't much more than five years old at the time. It was traumatic for those four boys and girl to rarely see their parents. Lorelle, the sensitive young daughter, couldn't handle it and ended up in a sanitarium due to her wild mood swings. Lorelle and President Kennedy's eldest sister, Rosemary, both underwent a frontal lobotomy around the same time. Morton and Joe Kennedy were friends. Both were Irishmen who had become very wealthy in America. The lobotomy procedure was not successful for either woman. At the time all this was happening, I was told that she had entered a nunnery. I had lost my cousin Lorelle forever. I never saw her again.

I'm not sure what the Kennedy kids were told. I can only imagine, since most of the Irish tend not to air their dirty laundry in public. This tragic connection in part brought Morton's family closer to the Kennedys. In fact, JFK actually lived in my uncle's house on Squaw Island, Hyannis Port while he was President. Morton's house was secluded—away from curious tourists—and thus easier for the Secret Service to guard the President there.

So, I totally understood why my cousins looked forward to Thanksgiving dinner with us year after year. They considered my nana to be their real mother. Bess cooked for them, listened to them, and cared for all of them. She was the eldest in the extended family and the grandmother who could be counted on to share her love with everyone.

Within days, I began to consider my near-death experience from my mother's perspective. I didn't want to question my mom or Aunt Shirley about what must have been an earth-shaking experience for them. My mother was very attentive to me when I was a child—not the type of person to allow her child to wander off near a swimming pool. At least, that's what I wanted to believe. I was her first-born child. I attributed her attentive behavior to the fact that she had lost her very first child in miscarriage—a fact I hadn't learned until I was well into adulthood.

Probably another reason for my mother not telling me the story of my drowning was the extreme sensitivity I exhibited as a child. During my pre-teen years, I sometimes felt intense emotional energy for no apparent reason. My body would occasionally begin to shake without warning. On one occasion, my family doctor was called to the house. He prescribed a sedative for anxiety. I took it for one day then stopped. Even as a ten-year-old, I knew that a kid shouldn't need medication when he could simply go outside and play. My family viewed me as the emotionally sensitive child and a worrywart. By age ten, the label had stuck. This, I believed, may have been a reason why my mother kept the drowning incident from me. Years later, I learned that exhibiting extreme sensitivity during childhood was very common among mediums. We are constantly absorbing energy from people and things around us.

During my early teens, I began to feel the same type of vibratory energy coming from individuals other than family members. Eventually this "energy experience" included actual information that I was able to interpret. I "knew" things but not understanding how I knew. I later came to understand that these were early psychic experiences.

I really don't know if there was a relationship between my near-death experience and the psychic events that began to unfold as I aged and matured. I have no recollection of my dying, or nearly dying. Many people who experience NDEs are able to recount amazing visions and stories from the other side, and their lives often change forever. I remembered nothing, but my life did begin to change forever. I began to see spirits. The near-death experience that I do have a vivid memory of wouldn't come until years later, when I suffered a heart attack and was met by a relative on the other side. I remember everything about *that* experience!

Some famous mediums have suggested to me that there is a relationship between the trauma of a near-death experience and the opening of psychic ability. Still other mediums are convinced that the gift of second sight is inherited from generation to generation. I believe that both explanations are probably valid. I had a mother who has admitted to objectively seeing full body apparitions of deceased spirits on many occasions. From my early teenage years, my mother has repeated the story of seeing "a man" sitting in the bedroom I shared with my two brothers. She was able to describe him but had no idea who he was. She spoke to him and he understood what she said to him—"Get out of the bedroom!"

The first time I heard her mention this experience was after dinner, in our living room. I was in my early teens, watching TV with the rest of the family. Mom blurted out that she had seen a man sitting on the edge of the bed in the back bedroom. Despite the noise from the set in the background, everyone heard her and turned away from the TV to look at Mom.

"What did you do when you saw him?" my brother asked.

"I yelled at him and asked what he was doing here. Then I told him to leave...and he stood right up and walked away," she said.

The room erupted in laughter. But it wasn't a joke. Mom was serious. It was that moment in the living room when I learned to keep my mouth shut about my visions and my sensitivities. The last thing I wanted was people laughing at me or thinking I was crazy. A few years later, Mom shared that she saw the same man in their Florida condo. Her clairvoyance continues today, into her tenth decade.

Believe me, I never wanted to be a psychic medium. This ability more or less "happened" to me and developed over many years. My near-death experience when I was two years old was only the first in a series of life-changing events. At age eight, I saw my first apparition. Soon thereafter, psychic experiences became commonplace. Looking back, I think I was always a clairvoyant who could see Spirit, but the feeling, sensing, knowing, and hearing developed over many years. Thankfully, these things didn't happen all at once. I probably couldn't have handled it.

Back then, I didn't share my experiences with anyone. I didn't want to be laughed at. Year after year, every paranormal experience got filed away to a place where I didn't have to think about it. Having learned that if a topic was too emotionally charged to discuss, then don't discuss it, I figured if I avoided my psychic experiences, then it would be as if they never happened. I became an expert at avoidance and keeping part of my life a secret. I lived two lives in two separate worlds and worked hard to keep those two worlds separate and apart.

But, as they say, truth is eventually revealed—Spirit kept knocking harder and harder at my door. My ability to *see* became coupled with *knowing* and *feeling* until I could no longer deny that something was happening to me. I could not turn away from who and what I was becoming. The other side continued pushing through and I had no idea why. I wasn't given a choice of whether or not to accept my ability. My ability accepted me. Mediumship was not a pastime activity or a hobby; it was what my soul had become.

3

My First Psychic Experience

Clairsentience: feeling the physical and emotional states of others

I was a sensitive child, but like most mediums, wasn't aware of why at the time. I was able to feel what was going on with friends and relatives, despite what their *words* were. I continued to believe that I wasn't any different than anyone else, nor did I want to be. It wasn't until information began to tag along with the energy feelings I received that I began to wonder about myself. I questioned whether I was normal. ("Normal" is the key word here. We all want to be normal, whatever that means.)

One Saturday in June of 1954, my great-uncle Morton Downey, the singer and actor, stopped by our house to visit his sister Bess, my grandmother. The night before, Morton had appeared on *The Eddie Fisher Show* on NBC in New York City. He had some free time before returning to Hollywood and wanted to visit with Bess, who I've mentioned shared in the raising of his five children, my cousins. Visits from Morton were quite rare, so when he was in town, the family became excited and wanted to see their famous relative. Bess was happy when Morton came around because she knew he'd be able to spend some rare time with his children.

Morton arrived that afternoon dressed formally in a black pinstripe suit and black shoes that shined like a mirror. His straight dark hair was cut and combed perfectly. His cologne had the room smelling like flowers. He looked like what he really was: a star. My parents, grandparents, brothers, sister, uncle, and my cousin Ann had all gathered in the living room that day to listen to our uncle talk about show business.

Morton always traveled with his agent, Jimmy Murphy. Jimmy was a very funny man whose job it was to warm up the audience prior to Morton's live performances in nightclubs. He was a natural at making people laugh.

Jimmy told us a story that day about the first time he went horseback riding. He was a short man who weighed at least three hundred pounds, so the thought of him sitting on a horse was funny, right from the start. I sat on the living-room floor and listened as he told us how his horse was extremely unhappy to be carrying all his weight.

"When I got up in the saddle, the horse just stands there. He wouldn't trot. So, I yelled and kicked at 'em," Jimmy shouted. Morton and my grandmother began to laugh. Jimmy spoke in an animated Irish accent that sounded as funny as his story.

"I kept yellin' and kickin'. Then the damn horse swings his neck around, looks at me with his big black eyes, and takes a bite outta-me-leg!" Jimmy screamed.

"Tell the kids what happened then," Morton shouted above the living room laughter.

"I bit 'em back," Jimmy yelled.

The room exploded in laughter. Screams filled the living room. I laughed even harder when I saw Morton give the Irish nod to his sister, Bess. That was his sign that Jimmy's story was absolutely true.

Jimmy, in an effort to keep his show going, took off his belt and threw it to my brother.

"How many of 'ye can fit inside me belt?" Jimmy asked.

My two brothers and I stood next to one another while Ann fastened the belt around the three of us. There was room to spare, so Ann attempted to squeeze herself inside the belt with us. Again, the room erupted.

For nearly twenty minutes, my attention was focused on Jimmy. The energy he created in the living room was palpable. This man had his audience in the palm of his hand. As I continued to watch him, seated on the living room sofa, a strange feeling overcame me. It lasted for a minute or so. I had watched Jimmy laugh uncontrollably yet I didn't *feel* that was who he really was. I was feeling something quite the opposite. The moment was confusing to me. My feeling and belief about him were in total contradiction to the humor everyone was experiencing. I knew absolutely nothing about Jimmy's life and had no information to base my feelings on. After all, I was just a nine-year-old kid who had just met him. I was having fun with my siblings and cousin, yet there was a different energetic feeling that I felt from Jimmy, an energy that did not match his happy personality. It was a *knowing* about Jimmy that was in total opposition to the comedy show I had just watched in my living room.

Jimmy was a comedian and entertainer who could command the attention of an audience. At the time, I didn't give much thought to the vast difference between what I saw and what I felt. I was a young kid. Not for a minute did I think that that was some kind of special ability. Not until years later, in a class with the famous medium, Mavis Pittilla, did I begin to accept that I had a psychic ability to pick up and interpret the energy of other individuals and to provide them with validation. (Later, I was able to do this in a controlled environment in which I was blindfolded.)

I didn't ask my mother for details about Jimmy's life until long after he had passed away. She didn't know much, apart from the show business work he did with Morton. (Apparently, he had many problems that were fueled by his alcohol abuse.) That early experience resonated with me for sixty years. It was powerful. As a child, I had no understanding of these energetic feelings. As a nine-year-old, I was busy with school, playing golf, and practicing my trombone. Another person's energy was the last thing on my mind. Like other emotionally charged events that had occurred, I had no reason to talk about them. Avoidance can make things go away, right? At least, that's what I thought.

4

LITTLE INDIAN BOY

Clairvoyancee: the ability to subjectively and objectively *see* those who have passed

A dairy farm, a pig farm, a chicken farm, and a mink ranch were all within walking distance of my front yard. I can't begin to tell you what the air smelled like during the hot and humid summer months when an east wind blew across our front yard. The women called it "nature's bouquet." The men called it "wind shit." My parents' house stood at the top of a hill overlooking a golf course built back in 1898, long before any homes lined the street. Our backyard was woodland. It was overgrown and "devoid of all life" except for a few rabbits and squirrels, but one afternoon, I found out that this had not always been the case.

In the spring of 1953, the year I turned eight, a bedroom was added to the rear of our house. One late afternoon, we came home after a backyard game of kick ball. My brothers went to watch TV, while I lay on my bed in our new bedroom, relaxing for awhile. The addition smelled of fresh lumber and was the closest I'd ever been to being inside a brand-new house.

I vividly remember lying on my back, legs crossed, hands grasped behind my head. I had that restful feeling that comes after cooling down from running around for an hour. My bed faced the rear window of our new room. The sun cast long afternoon shadows through the pine trees in the backyard.

Out of the blue, a small dark-haired boy dressed in a light-brown suede shirt appeared at the window. I moved toward the edge of my bed, thinking it was a shadow. The image of the boy remained. My next thought was, *maybe it's Chris* (our next-door neighbor). He sometimes wore a Davy Crockett suede shirt when he played in his yard. But it didn't make sense. Chris had blonde hair and was only about four feet tall. Someone would have to be *eight feet tall* to look directly into the new bedroom window. This boy had light brown skin and American Indian features. I continued to gaze in his direction. I was not in the least bit frightened and was rather more curious than anything else. Somehow, my vision was accompanied by a peaceful feeling. The apparition of this young boy occurred two more times during the summer and fall, but I never mentioned it to anyone. Again, I kind of forgot about the whole thing due to my reluctance to talk about it. I was beginning to get very good at avoidance. Silence was golden—at least until I reached the fifth grade.

I was ten years old at the time and a bit slow in getting moving as I was recovering from having had my appendix removed. I had to stay around the house to allow the eight-inch incision on my lower abdomen to heal. As my appendix had nearly ruptured, the surgeon had to make an extra-long incision. (Arthroscopic surgery was not available in 1955.) I was cut and stapled like my grandmother's pot roast. As a result, I couldn't do much of anything. Playing golf, playing my trombone—everything was out of the question until my cut muscles healed. The only activity I was able to do was the homework sent home with my younger brothers.

That fall, a log cabin playhouse was delivered to our backyard. It was the most awesome present we had ever received. It was an early Christmas gift from a wealthy man who was a very good friend of my father. It would be large enough for all four of us kids to sleep in it, and we looked forward to camping in our new "fort." My Gramp Ed agreed to take on the project to put the cabin together. The floor had to be set into the ground for support, so our job was to dig the foundation. I had dug down about a foot when my shovel hit something hard. I thought, *Stones?* but realized quickly that it wasn't.

"Look! These are arrowheads!" I shouted to my brothers.

We each grabbed an arrowhead to inspect. We rubbed our fingers across the chiseled surfaces in silence. We understood that we had found a piece of history, right in our backyard. The arrowheads were about two inches long and still remarkably sharp. The middle of each one was thick, with smooth crevices on either side. They seemed to have been chipped out of stone. We looked at one another in utter surprise. In that moment, we became aware that this was Indian land. We were not the first people to have lived here. We had learned in school that Indians lived in Connecticut, but coming face to face with the evidence was humbling.

It wasn't until about a year later, when I was eleven, that I found myself alone in the backyard where I had dug up the arrowheads. I couldn't help but wonder if there was a connection between the Indian boy I had seen a few times and the arrowheads. Over three years had passed since my first vision of him at my bedroom window. But I pushed the thought aside and chose not to spend time trying to figure out something I couldn't understand or prove. Again, I chose to forget about the whole thing.

5

Store-Front Psychic

"The psychic lady wore a purple turban and sat in a basement window, smoking a cigarette."

—J. Deary, Manhattan, 1959

Who doesn't remember the first time they visited New York City? I was fourteen. The hundred-mile drive to Manhattan in the family Oldsmobile was not a sightseeing trip. My father was taking me to Manhattan's Garment District to get new clothes for my first day at the Catholic prep school I had been accepted into. As he had a friend in the business, that meant wholesale prices—Dad never liked to pay retail. As I am sure you recall, he was a highly educated man who instilled in his children the importance of hard work, an education, and being thrifty with their hard-earned cash. The primary reason for the long drive to Manhattan was to save money. My father was the son of an Irish immigrant and at a very young age, was sent out onto the streets of Boston to sell hard-boiled eggs for a penny apiece. (At least, as I explained earlier, that was the repeating story we heard every time we complained about anything.)

Dad had won scholarships to prep school, college, graduate school, and law school, so it was a given that one day I, too, would have to compete for similar financial assistance. I took the scholarship entrance exam for the world-famous Choate School early in 1959. In addition to being a pretty good student, I was an excellent golfer. By thirteen, I had already won my first silver trophy. My trombone lessons had paid off, and I was the youngest member of the town orchestra. My folks thought that my academic, athletic, and musical abilities would at least get me an invitation to sit for the scholarship. They believed I was the kind of well-rounded student who could win a scholarship. But a friend of mine won the scholarship that year—I came in second. So, I was accepted into Choate School, but sadly, not on scholarship. Choate was and still remains one of the most expensive private schools in the world. Enough said!

Fairfield Prep was my private school fallback option. It was a Catholic boys' school taught by Jesuit priests about forty miles from where I lived. My father had been Jesuit educated and turned out to be a successful guy, so he wanted me to have the same opportunity. Prior to his work in the FBI, Dad had worked on Madison Avenue in advertising, and later on, for Coca-Cola. Looking back, I guess I wanted to be as successful as he was. I was very fortunate to have the opportunity to attend private school.

The Jesuits had a strict dress code for all students. A sports jacket, white shirt, and tie were the uniform of the day. So, off we went to New York City. Dad wasn't bothered by the two-hundred-mile round-trip journey as he would save a bundle of cash in the Garment District.

Our shopping day in New York City proved more fun than I had imagined. Dad told stories of his days working in Manhattan in advertising prior to joining the FBI. He drove us by the Chelsea Hotel on 23rd Street where he had lived. Years later, I learned that Mark Twain, Dylan Thomas, Tennessee Williams, Jack Kerouac, Allen Ginsberg, and Bob Dylan (to name a few), had all lived at the Chelsea Hotel. I thought that was very cool! Dad, however, was a very private kind of guy. He never spoke about his investigative work in the Bureau. His work was always a secret, and like many who work in national intelligence, Dad lived two lives. He was an expert at avoiding talking about what happened to him every day on the job. This was difficult to deal with when I was a kid. After all, most school children talked with their dads about what they did day in and day out. Many school kids plan to follow in their father's footsteps as firemen, lawyers, doctors, or whatever. I had absolutely no idea what my father did. When asked by friends, I had no answer. Years later, as an adult, I learned a great deal about the nature of FBI work from my brother, who did follow in Dad's footsteps. Only then did I understand the danger involved and why he didn't want to talk about his work.

That particular day, the magic of Manhattan came alive. We parked in midtown near Seventh Avenue and walked into a large warehouse. My father's friend, who owned a wholesale loft in the garment district, sold men's clothing to department stores all over the country from the top floor of a warehouse almost the size of a football field. It was off limits to the general public. My mother always reminded us kids that our dad knew a lot of people due to his position in the FBI. Having a friend, one-hundred miles away, who sold clothing nationwide, really confirmed that for me. The place was wall-to-wall with suits and sport coats.

"Are you looking for an American, European, Country Western, or French-cut jacket?" the man asked. I tried my best not to act like a tourist. Nobody in Manhattan wants to look like a tourist.

"I'll take a look at some European-cut sports jackets," I replied. My mother glanced over at me.

"How do you know about European-cut jackets?" she asked.

"I saw them in *Playboy Magazine*," I joked. She glared at me with a creased brow.

"I can't wait till those Jesuits get ahold of you," she struck back.

The salesman wheeled in two racks of sports coats from the back of the warehouse. I chose three jackets and a few ties. My dad selected some ties before we headed to lunch at Horn & Hardart cafeteria. Twenty-five years later, my business partners and I would be responsible for providing health care to all Garment District employees. Funny how those synchronicities happen.

During the short walk down Seventh Avenue, we passed by four or five small basement shops with bright neon signs in the window that read "Psychic Readings." In one window, a lady with a purple turban sat on a sofa, smoking a cigarette. She apparently lived and worked in the same little room. Every psychic we passed was female. They looked like caricatures with black hair, pale skin, and some sort of covering on their heads. I pretty much understood what psychics did for a living.

Even then, as a young teen, I felt I could probably do what they did, if I really wanted to.

I guess I always believed that there was something sacred in connecting with another person's soul. It hit me hard that my strange ability could have me sitting behind a storefront window in a seedy section of Times Square—I never wanted to end up sitting in a storefront window, doing that type of work. *Psychics should be able to have an honorable profession*, I thought. Could you imagine a man like my father learning that his eldest son was a Broadway Psychic? I know, but back then, it wasn't funny. Today, I have a different view about psychic ability and how it's an ability that can change people's lives for the better. Today, I understand how a psychic can use a crystal ball to "get out of their minds" to focus. But that day, back in 1959, I didn't like what I saw.

6

Three Priests

"We all have our crosses to bear."

—Christian saying

"All aboard!" the engineer yelled at the top of his lungs. When I heard that shout, I knew my day had begun. The grogginess that accompanied getting up at sunrise every morning was beginning to disappear. With books under my arm, I boarded the train for my early morning ride to prep school. The tuition at the Catholic Jesuit prep school was only a fraction of the $50,000 tuition for Choate School. Unfortunately, attending the Catholic school required a daily, seventy-two-mile round trip train ride to the other end of Connecticut.

Every morning, I searched the train for a double seat so I could sleep for the hour ride down the Connecticut coastline. It was not a scenic ride. The Gold Coast politicians had ensured the train tracks were never laid anywhere near the beautiful private beaches and mansions owned by some of the wealthiest people in the country. Most of the coastline was off-limits to the families who lived in adjacent towns.

I slept lightly, only to be disturbed by businessmen on the way into Manhattan's financial and advertising centers. I felt sorry for those guys. They were doomed to make this trip until retirement—the commuter "life sentence." I looked forward to being released from the daily train ride after high school. Little did I realize at the time that I too would be doomed to ride the commuter train for many years of my life until retirement.

The daily commute was tiring. Actually, it was boring, but as a kid I didn't know the difference between tired and bored. I'm not sure there is one.

I woke up at six o'clock every day. Rather, my mother woke me up. She was already busy making me scrambled eggs for breakfast. By seven o'clock, she drove me to the train station to catch the seven twenty-five. I never appreciated her dedication to my schedule till much later in life. I was her daily morning routine and she never complained.

The train ride was lonely and loud. The wheels scratched and banged along iron rails that were long overdue for a facelift. As one of my Jesuit teachers reminded me, "We all have our cross to bear." Everyone has heard that phrase before, but how many received the message firsthand from a Jesuit priest just off the boat from the Vatican? Those words definitely had a biblical flair that stuck with me forever.

During childhood, most of us have had things happen that we didn't completely understand. That's how life happens on the journey to adulthood. Later on, a light bulb gets turned on and we experience our aha moments when everything becomes clear. What I'm about to write about was *not one of those occasions*. To this day, I have no idea or understanding of the reason or meaning behind the experience—though I do have a working theory that I'll share.

One particular morning during my sophomore year still quite vividly stands out in my memory. A half-hour before the lunch bell, a loud knock on the classroom door jolted everyone in Latin class. Father Higgins stopped reading about Caesar's conquest of Gaul and turned toward the door with a scowl on his face. No one, and I mean *no one* ever interrupted Father Higgins when he was teaching Latin. What on Earth couldn't wait thirty more minutes until lunch break? As he opened the door, I could see three priests standing out in the hallway. Unlike Higgins, who always wore a black cassock, theirs were colorful. Higgins walked back to his desk, his eyes focused directly on me. My heart began to race.

"Mr. Deary, there are three priests here to see you," he said in his distinct Boston accent.

My already-racing heart started to pound in my chest. My face turned beet-red. Three priests! *Why? What did I do?* I asked myself.

Three Priests

Frightened, I stood up and headed to the hallway. I was in a nervous daze and could hear catcalls and laughter from my classmates. I was not amused. I was on my own.

"Deary must be in *trouble*," one boy whispered. In what felt like a slow-motion march, I reached the hallway. Not one of the three priests introduced themselves. I thought it odd, but in the moment, I was too scared to care. The conversation began abruptly.

"How are you doing today, Mr. Deary?" the priest to my right asked.

"Fine, Father," I replied. *How do they know my name? And why are they here?* I wondered.

"What kind of sports do you like?" the priest continued.

My mind went blank. I was filled with anxiety. I didn't know why I was there. To say the conversation was awkward was an understatement. *These priests got me out of class to ask me about sports?* My thoughts jumped around.

"I like swimming," I coughed out from my dry throat.

In my nervous anxiety, I had totally gone blank about the fact that I was one of the better young golfers in the state. I felt scared and ridiculous. *Who are these men and why am I here? Am I in trouble?* I kept asking myself. I had never seen them before. Clearly, they did not teach at the prep school. The school shared its campus with a Jesuit university. *Maybe that's where they came from,* I thought.

Two of the priests wore white with their cassock while the older priest was dressed much differently. He wore white and gold and appeared to be much more formal. He stood to my left and listened quietly as I mumbled one-word answers to the questions thrown at me; questions that appeared to have no relevance to anything.

Despite the large empty hallway where we stood, the three priests were very close to me, too close, in fact. I was uncomfortable and felt surrounded by the three of them. Up until that point, only one priest had spoken to me. The other two seemed to be studying me. I could feel their energy and in a strange way, I knew they were connected to me. It was not unlike the energy I now feel and can recognize as an adult psychic and medium. The older priest turned toward me. We locked eyes.

"Are you staying close to God?" he asked. I didn't have time to think.

"Yes, Father," I blurted out. He nodded his head in affirmation.

Without another word the three turned and walked away. No goodbyes, no explanations, no names...nothing! I returned to my seat. My head screamed, *Are you kidding me? What just happened? Was I getting thrown out of school?* I wanted an explanation. I needed an explanation. I waited in the classroom with Father Higgins while my friends headed for lunch in the cafeteria.

"Father Higgins, who were those three priests?" I finally got to ask.

Higgins, standing behind his desk organizing papers, didn't look up, but said they had "something to do with the university." Clearly, he didn't want to discuss this any further. I left to join my friends for lunch.

I later came up with a theory about what might have happened that day. It never really gave me total closure, but it was a possible explanation that I could live with.

Weeks before the three priests showed up at my classroom door, every student throughout the school was given a surprise in-class assignment. Everyone was allowed a half-hour to write their personal feelings about the Nature of Man. No explanation was given. It had nothing to do with philosophy because we had yet to study religion or philosophy.

I remember not being confused about the assignment as much as others in the class seemed. I wrote quickly. The words and ideas flowed quite easily from pen to paper. I wrote about philosophical issues that I had not yet studied. Looking back, I think I wrote with an understanding that may have been beyond the grasp of most fourteen-year-olds. Don't get me wrong...I was never a great writer so it was definitely not an intellectually astute composition. It was more of an awareness and understanding of life and belief in a higher power that the other students were likely unable to write about.

Some time later, one of the students in the lunchroom asked if anyone had received a grade on the assignment. Everyone was silent. It seemed that no one had had their assignment returned. And no one else had received a visit from the three priests. Did something I wrote that day give these guys the idea that I was a candidate for a life in the monastery? If so, how could I have been the only one? I'll never know.

I've thought about that encounter many times over the years and the significance of why only two of the priests spoke. The third priest was intense and silent. He felt like a psychic, reading the soul of another. His energy was palpable.

Based upon some of the psychic and mediumistic abilities I have now as an adult, it's an explanation I can live with. The priest may have been checking me psychically to see if I was suitable for their profession. Many priests and nuns in religious orders have this sensitivity and ability. As explained to me once by Mavis Pittilla, "Three hundred years ago all of us mediums would have been rounded up and placed into a monastery."

I know, a wild and crazy assumption and theory, some may say. Well, this experience pales in comparison to some of the other things that happened on my path toward accepting my ability as a psychic and medium.

I never saw those three priests again. To this day, I am left only with the possibility that one of those priests had a psychic ability to see a psychic sensitivity in me that I was not yet aware of.

7
Two Faces of Evil

Clairsentience: the ability to perceive psychic energy
that is imperceptible to the five senses

The Civil Rights Movement was in full swing during 1967—the year I moved to Georgia. I didn't know exactly what I was getting myself into by moving south of the Mason-Dixon line. Up until then, "civil rights" was only a term I had heard on the evening news. I was ready for a change of climate so decided to leave college in Massachusetts and continue in Georgia. A move to the south sounded like an adventure. In fact, it proved to be even more than that.

I was a thousand miles from home and totally on my own—an experience and a freedom that every kid waits for in their life. I soon learned that total independence from family is a two-edged sword. There was no going home for the weekend, or even holidays for that matter. I was a Yankee from New England living in the Deep South during the reign of segregation. The 1964 federal legislation meant to end segregation didn't seem to matter in the rural south. Many of the students I met had great-grandparents who had told them stories of their homes being burned during General Sherman's March to Savannah. Even the words "Civil War" were not used by the southerners I knew. Instead, it was referred to as "the war of northern aggression." I had a lot to learn and not all of it was pleasant. Despite the problems I encountered, I loved the south and in a strange way felt more at home there than I had in New England.

My newly adopted home was a hotbed of racial injustice. African Americans had just recently been allowed entrance to the state university. Despite the new laws that repealed segregation, I saw very few Black students on campus. The university continued the separation of the races with designated "Black Only" restrooms and "Black Only" drinking fountains. Black students were absolutely forbidden to eat in any of the downtown restaurants. Segregation meant that I could not go out to eat with any of my African American friends from New York. Segregation, for me, had become more than an abstract word. It was personal.

"We're headed to the boarding house restaurant tonight for dinner. They have peach pie on Thursday night. You want to come with me and Ringo?" I asked Beau one night.

My roommate, Ringo, stood in sharp contrast to Beau, who was a foot taller and weighed twice as much. Ringo, however, had a personality that towered above most people. With his cowboy boots, silver rodeo buckle, and Levi jeans, Ringo was an impressive guy on campus. Ringo and I had met Beau earlier that week in the student center. He was an African American transfer student from Harlem. "No. I'll get something from the machine at the student center," Beau said.

"Come on. It's all-you-can-eat at the boarding house," I said.

"I can't go into that white honky place. They'd never serve a Black man. Trust me, I know," Beau said.

"He's probably right," Ringo said.

For the first time in my life, I felt the sharp edge of internal rage. I didn't know how to deal with the anger I felt. Imagine that you had plans to go out to dinner with a friend but find out that you are "not allowed." Then imagine that if you disobeyed the local rules, you may be *jailed or suffer bodily harm*. Now imagine that there's absolutely *nothing you can do about it*. Months later, a group of us students did attempt to do something about it. An organization associated with a Baptist preacher in Atlanta named Reverend Martin Luther King organized a non-violent sit-in protest at the university. The sad result of our non-violent sit-in was that segregation continued and we were suspended from the university for ten weeks. Upon our return to campus, we tried to make the best of a bad situation. There were plans for more demonstrations in the south.

One hot day, we did our best to relax and get away from all the segregation we had been experiencing. We drove deep into the countryside to a cold-water creek. Ringo turned off of the paved highway and onto a dusty road that had been carved through the middle of a cotton field by tractor wheels. The muffler of Ringo's 1955 Chevy banged each time it bottomed out onto the Georgia red clay. The worn-out whitewall tires shook the steering wheel back and forth as we bounced between the road ruts.

We parked alongside the bank of the creek at the end of the road. Ringo and Beau got out and ran, fully dressed, into the water. I waited in the car for the dust to settle, then changed into a pair of swim shorts. I held my nose and jumped into the deep end where the two of them were floating on their backs. The sun was Georgia hot but the water was cold. We had the place all to ourselves. Like kids, we exhausted ourselves by sliding on our backsides over and over down the water-worn rocks that dropped us into the deep-water creek. It was a good kind of tired and for a moment, all was right with the world.

Before we knew it, the sun was disappearing behind the cotton field, signaling that it was time to begin our drive back to the university. Ringo had found the out-in-the-middle-of-nowhere swimming hole during daylight hours, so finding our way home after dark through unmarked backcountry dirt roads would be another story.

As we headed back to the Chevy, we noticed a cloud of Georgia-red clay dust above the cotton field about a half-mile away. A white Ford pick-up truck drove out of the sunset directly toward us—the road was so narrow we knew we had to wait for them to pass before we could leave. The dust cloud got closer and closer.

"Why's this guy in such a big hurry? The swimming hole ain't going nowhere," Ringo said.

Beau and I looked at each other. In a split-second our expressions changed to serious. As the truck pulled up in front of our Chevy, trapping us at the creek, I caught a glimpse of the driver.

"Oh shit!" I yelled, my skin crawling.

The driver's door bolted open, and a large man jumped out from behind the wheel as his sidekick grabbed a shotgun from the gun rack. Both men were dressed in long white robes— black crosses painted on the left side of their chests. White hoods hung down and back across their shoulders, leaving their faces clearly exposed.

This is not good, I thought to myself.

The men stopped and stood directly in front of us, about fifteen feet away. The double-barrel shotgun was aimed directly at my head. It's a moment I'll never forget. My mind went blank—all thoughts just disappeared. It was one of those moments when I was too scared to be afraid. As if by instinct, Ringo, Beau, and I moved slowly away from one another in a weak attempt to make us a wider target.

"What y'all doing here?" the driver barked.

"Just swimming," I blurted out. My mind began to race—*the middle of nowhere. Alone. Beau is Black.* A few years earlier, the Ku Klux Klan had killed some Black students along with their white friends in nearby Alabama. All I could think about during my paralysis of fear was *these guys weren't hiding their faces*. There could be reasons for that that I was not ready to consider.

Despite all that was happening, I had an overwhelming feeling that we would come out of the situation alive. It didn't make any sense, but my fear vanished. I somehow *just knew* that none of us were going to die that day. This *knowing* was strong enough to keep me calm during the life-and-death situation. I didn't feel that these guys were killers, but having a shotgun aimed at my head by a member of the Ku Klux Klan definitely had my attention.

"Where ya' from?" the driver asked.

My mind continued to race. I didn't want to admit that I was a Yankee. But I was pretty sure this guy had already seen the New York State tag on the Chevy.

"We're students from the university. We're Georgia Bulldogs," I said in an attempt to make a connection.

"What about the nigger?" he asked.

The sound of that word echoed with hate and immediately, all attention was focused on Beau. I swallowed hard. Beau took a step back, fearing the worst. I knew from his question that this guy had no idea that Georgia schools had been integrated and that Blacks could now attend. The other Klansman turned the gun away from me and pointed it at Beau. We all froze.

"NO! He's a student, too," I shouted quickly. I didn't want them focused on Beau.

The men glanced at each other. It became even more evident that these guys had no idea that the federal government had ended segregation. Or maybe they didn't care.

"He's gotta' get out of here," the man said, the gun still aimed at Beau.

We wasted no time moving toward the Chevy.

"Wait a minute!" the guy with the gun shouted. We stopped in our tracks. Our hearts pounded.

"You white boys can stay here," he said in a matter-of-fact tone.

"It's getting dark. We better get going," I said.

The two men jumped quickly into their truck and drove back into the cotton field. We watched as the truck's red-dust cloud faded into a pink sunset.

Overcome with nervous exhaustion, no one said a word until we were out of the cotton field.

"You guys okay?" I asked.

"We're all alone out here. We're in the middle of nowhere. How in hell did the Klan know I was here?" Beau asked. Ringo and I shook our heads. Beau's question filled me with rage and made me want to cry.

We could have been killed! Thank God I was right about those guys, I thought to myself. *We're a long way from civilization. No one would have missed us if we disappeared. The few people we know on campus would have figured we were still suspended from the university and living back home up north. I trusted my instinct. I actually bet my life on it. This knowing is stronger than an instinct. I can't explain it and don't need to...not today anyway. We're alive.*

I don't remember seeing much of Beau after that day. Our classes were at opposite ends of the campus. Ringo and I never spoke again about what had happened. We had experienced a kind of trauma and there really was no one to talk to about it. Again, avoidance seemed like a reasonable way to handle it. Back then, who would have listened anyway?

Sadly, a few months later, we weren't surprised to learn that Dr. King had been assassinated in Tennessee. We knew firsthand about the hate that some had toward people of color.

I remember that day well…especially the sadness…but also the *knowing*.

8

MEDIUM IN THE GEORGIA MOUNTAINS

"You have the 'clear eyes.'"

—Mada Love, 1967

One day, Ringo asked if we wanted to drive up into the mountains of North Georgia. He wanted Greek, our roommate, and I to keep him company. Truth was, he had more laughs when we were around. In fact, all of us laughed when we were together. Ringo had traveled up to the mountain lake a week earlier and admittedly, was bored being up there alone. The mountains would also give us a break from the late-summer humidity.

Greek and Ringo had shared a house for a few months before inviting me in. We met in class and hit it off immediately. There was constant humor—the laughs were nonstop. We had the ability to be an audience for and play off of one another. I learned from them how to view the world from a less serious perspective. In 1967, we were dealing with segregation, racism, illegal rules, unenforced integration law, tornadoes, and a war surging in Southeast Asia. Oh, and did I mention, no air conditioning? (It wasn't until 1970 that air conditioning units made it into American homes.) We live on Earth, not in heaven. However, Georgia in the summertime without air conditioning definitely resembles hell. In any event, my point is, laughter helps during terrible times.

Greek really was a Greek. I think I was the only one who actually knew his real name— thirty letters long. He didn't have the patience to continually repeat the spelling of his first, middle and last names to his friends, so he simply became The Greek. He was well known on campus due to his cultural heritage and his humor. He would often approach a pretty girl, speak Greek to her while appearing lost and confused, gain her sympathy...and a date. He would usually crack up laughing before the girl realized it was a dating scam. As far as I knew, he was the only authentic Greek at the university at that time. Sorority girls were intrigued with the quiet, good-looking, dark-haired fellow of European descent. And, like Ringo, he shared his humor with everyone.

Ringo's invitation for a weekend out of town caught my attention. The southern heat and humidity had begun to blanket the countryside around Atlanta. I've traveled far and wide but have yet to find humidity as thick as that of central Georgia in the summertime. Some say the rain is dryer than the humidity in Georgia. We understood why the locals named the city, "Hot-lanta."

"It's a lot cooler up in the mountains," Ringo had said.

"I suppose I'll go. Nothing much to do around here this weekend," Greek replied.

"I met a woman up there. She was very interesting," Ringo added. Greek and I looked at each other. We knew there was more to this journey than Ringo was letting on.

"We are not going up to the mountains to accompany you on a *date*," Greek growled.

"No. No, she's an older woman. She's in her sixties and a very nice lady. She told me to bring my friends the next time I visit. She calls herself Mada Love," Ringo said.

"What kind of name is that?" Greek asked.

"What kind of name has thirty letters in it?" I laughed back.

"I guess we can go. As long as it's not some kind of Holy Roller meeting," I said. Greek groaned in agreement. On the seventy-mile drive to North Georgia, Ringo explained that Mada Love was some type of holy person.

"She lives alone in a large Victorian house. Nearby are a few smaller houses where she holds meetings," Ringo said.

"What kind of meetings?" Greek asked.

"Interesting discussions," Ringo replied.

During 1967, the social culture of Georgia remained relatively conservative. The age of hippies, communes, psychedelic music, and drugs had not yet taken its transforming hold on American society. The "Summer of Love" cultural phenomenon was still months away. As calm as everything was in America, it was downright sleepy in rural Georgia.

"Someone told me she is a psychic medium," Ringo admitted as he parked the car, hours later, near Lake Rabun.

"You mean she's a fortune teller?" I asked. My mind shot back to the psychics with their crystal balls and turbans in Times Square.

"No. It's nothing weird. I've been here before. It'll be fun," Ringo replied.

Greek released another moan of disinterest. I had no idea what a psychic medium was. I think it was the first time I had ever heard that term. I had heard the word psychic but medium was new to me. I couldn't imagine why Ringo was interested in driving seventy miles into the mountains of North Georgia to visit one. But Ringo was always open to new ideas, so we were all in.

And, he was right: by the time we had reached Lake Rabun, the temperature had dropped dramatically and the humidity was bearable. We jumped out, immediately joined a small group of people waiting outside, then walked with them across a long lawn to a small building adjacent to Mada's large Victorian house. Most were about our age but didn't look like university students. Something about them was different.

"Why isn't anyone talking?" Greek whispered.

"Everyone stays pretty quiet around Mada Love," Ringo said.

"Being quiet must be extremely difficult for you, Ringo," I joked.

We had entered a small white dome structure made of cinder blocks and concrete. The white dome stood in sharp contrast to the pine-covered hills and deep-blue summer sky. The ceiling inside was very low and was about twenty feet across. Twelve of us sat in a circle on the concrete floor. Ringo and Greek sat cross-legged on each side of me.

"Two weeks ago, there were only six of us here," Ringo said.

Greek and I looked at one another—Ringo had conveniently forgotten to tell us that we had to sit cross-legged in a dome. I'm sure he was afraid that had we known, we wouldn't have agreed to come. He would have been correct.

"Last time I was here, Mada Love said that it's best if thirteen people participate together in the circle. She didn't say why," Ringo said.

A few minutes later, an older woman entered the dome and took her seat within the circle, directly across from me. Mada Love looked to be the age of my grandmother. She had grey-white hair, was about average height, and was a little overweight. There were no introductions. Within moments she took a black stone object from a small, red, suede bag.

"This is black quartz from Tibet. I would like each of you to hold the stone in your left hand for a few moments. Speak whatever words come to your mind when you receive the stone. Then pass it to the person on your left," she said.

Greek and I looked at each other again. We clearly shared the "no interest in being part of this exercise" feeling. Everyone else, including Ringo, was taking this exercise very seriously. Greek and I were bored out of our minds. I listened to each person speak a few words after they had been handed the black stone. Their remarks ranged from "thank you for this opportunity" to "this is a peaceful place." Others passed the stone along to the next person without saying a word. I had made up my mind to join the avoidant group and say nothing. I wanted to remain silent and get this over with as quickly as possible. Ringo turned toward me and placed the stone in my left hand. I accepted it reluctantly. I made sure he saw the frustration on my face. I closed my fingers around the small black stone. It was very cold despite having been held by six or seven other people.

"Self-realization through self-actualization," I blurted out.

I was stunned. Everyone's eyes were suddenly on me. The words had jumped out of my mouth...and they had been *loud*. I'm not a loud person. I hadn't planned on saying a thing. How could my voice speak when my plan was to keep quiet, like most of the others? How could I speak words that *meant absolutely nothing* to me? Greek made his "nervous cough sound" that he used to hide inappropriate laughter. I passed it to him and continued to listen as the rest of the people took their turn with the stone. Within minutes, the black stone was back into the hands of Mada Love. Everyone sat in quiet anticipation.

"What now?" Greek whispered. Ringo said nothing. His eyes were closed like he was meditating.

Mada sat motionless for minutes with her eyes closed as well. It felt like an eternity. Greek and I were restless. We were more than ready to get out of there. Finally, Mada opened her eyes. She looked across the room, directly at me, and stared into my eyes.

"You have lived many lives," she said when she finally spoke.

Oh no, I thought to myself. The group wasn't sure where her message was directed, but I knew immediately that she was speaking to me—Greek and Ringo knew too.

"At least four of your lives were lived as a priest," she continued.

As she spoke, my thoughts seemed to leave me. I was completely focused on her. I felt a kind of magnetic energy that pulled at me with a physical sensation. Later, it dawned on me that what I felt was not unlike what I had experienced in the past on many occasions: the time in my living room with Jimmy Murphy, the time with the three priests at prep school, the time at the cold-water creek with Beau. This was the same *energy feeling* I had experienced throughout my life.

Mada's attention turned back to the group. She concluded with a few remarks about her trip to South Carolina to visit with an Iranian mystic named Meher Baba. She explained that Meher Baba had chosen not to speak for almost forty years. She said his energy filled the room when he entered it. She had experienced an extremely peaceful and healing effect when she was in his presence. This was the first time I had ever heard someone speak about experiencing the energy of another person. She had my full attention—she had said she was able to *feel* the energy of a person. A few years later while in England, I was fortunate enough to learn what Mada Love meant when she said, "his energy filled the room."

In 1971, I had the opportunity to visit with an Indian holy man who had traveled to Bristol, England from the Golden Temple in Punjab, India to visit with his followers. The man was said to be from the lineage of Guru Nanak, a spiritual leader of the Sikh religion. When I walked into the small room to meet him, I was asked by one of his followers if I had any questions. I said no—I was speechless. I felt the energy of this man's presence. Time stood still. I was basking in the energy of his peace. I experienced an energy similar to that described by Mada Love when she met with Meher Baba.

Mada finished speaking and invited everyone into her home for lunch.

"Free lunch! That's the reason Ringo likes coming up here to the Georgia mountains," I said to Greek.

Mada served finger sandwiches and iced tea. The food presentation was refined and very southern. Her living room was decorated in Victorian style—white lace covered the arms of the chairs and decorative pillows were placed on the love seats. A black cat wandered around, brushing his tail against everyone in the room.

One of the men who took care of the property told me that Mada was constantly having spirit visitations. He described how he himself had seen spirits sitting on the sofa with her. *Why is this man telling me these supernatural stories?* I wondered. I was polite but didn't respond. I vividly remember thinking, *there must be something seriously wrong with this guy.* I walked over and grabbed the pitcher of iced tea, pouring one for Mada as well. Her comment about my having been a priest still echoed in my head. I'm generally a shy person but I decided to question her about what she had said.

"How many more lives do I have to live?" I joked.

"Very many," Mada replied. She saw the look of disappointment on my face.

"Four lives as a priest just didn't do it?" I smiled.

"You have 'the clear eyes,' " she said in a very serious tone then moved to the middle of the dining area. I stood there, trying to make sense of what she had said. She raised her voice to address everyone in the room. I held onto my cup of tea nervously.

"Many of you here today died during the Second World War," she said in a matter-of-fact tone. Ringo looked over at me and shrugged his shoulders. Then, with a big smile, he saluted proudly in my direction.

Mada Love's words had such an impact on me that I've never forgotten that afternoon with her. Her statements about four lives as a priest, having the clear eyes, and reincarnation from World War II, continue to resonate with me.

Not until my late forties did I understand that "clear eyes" was in reference to the word clairvoyant. The word is French in origin and refers to the psychic ability to clearly see beyond the natural range of the human senses. Mada Love was telling me that I was a clairvoyant. She was letting me know that I had an ability to "see" beyond the physical world.

Apparently, she chose not to discuss any specific details of my ability with me that day. Looking back, I know I would not have been receptive to that type of information. She was able to somehow see and know that I had the same ability as she did. Today, I can often see this ability in others.

In 1967, "psychic" was not a phenomenon familiar to the general population. This was especially true in the rural South. While that Saturday at Lake Rabun had captured my imagination, it was not something I wanted to explore further. Generally, I don't dwell on things that I don't understand. Again, I used avoidance to handle the situation. I never returned to Lake Rabun.

During the next ten months, both Martin Luther King and Bobby Kennedy were assassinated. Serious social and political issues erupted in America. College students began to get involved in movements aimed at putting an end to racism, sexism, and nuclear war. Discussing past lives and psychics made for interesting conversation but for me was not grounded in the reality of those turbulent times.

9

Haunted by the Past

"The distinction between past, present, and future is only a stubbornly persistent illusion."

—Albert Einstein, 1955

Prior to my mid-twenties, I knew absolutely nothing about the Nazi SS occupation of the Netherlands. Little did I know that I was destined to learn quite a bit about it. Following my graduation from college and a brief trip to the Soviet Ukraine with my girlfriend, I settled in Amsterdam. The freedom I experienced in the Netherlands was in sharp contrast to my week in Russia where every move we made was under the watchful eye of the KGB. In 1970, a Cold War was being waged between the USA and Russia. The fact that my girlfriend spoke Ukrainian and my father was a special agent with the FBI didn't go well with our Russian hosts. Frankly, they wondered what we were doing in their country. A connection with the FBI and someone who spoke Russian more often than not meant foreign spy, but our lives were far removed from the world of James Bond!

I rented a houseboat on the Amstel River not far from the Anne Frank House. The Amsterdam houseboat community was an interesting array of European artists, musicians, and American ex-patriots. Each morning I woke to freezing Arctic air blowing through the cracks in the deck of my houseboat. The potbelly stove held enough coal to keep me warm for about six hours, so I normally slept from midnight to 6:00 a.m. When I say it was freezing in the morning—on more than one morning, the Heineken beer on my table was frozen in the bottle.

The Dutch are a very kind and almost carefree group of people. With its canal boats, flower markets, and cobblestone streets, Amsterdam quickly became my favorite European city. I actually considered relocating there permanently.

I soon became aware of some minor discomfort during my morning walks past the Anne Frank House. I remembered from high school history class that during the Nazi occupation of the Netherlands, the Frank family had been forced into hiding into an attic in one of the buildings where Anne's father, Otto, worked. He was the only survivor of the Frank family. However, the strange bodily sensation I had was not related to any of the sadness I felt for their family. It was different—a physical sensation. I had visited every tourist site in Amsterdam during the years I lived there, but for some reason couldn't get myself to go inside the Anne Frank House. What I felt, I could not put a name to. However, the feeling and sensation were strong enough to keep me away from the Anne Frank House on the mornings that I walked along the Prinsengracht Canal.

Not unlike my feelings about the Anne Frank House, I also never cared to walk through Amsterdam's Dam Square despite it being the shortest route to the railroad station. I felt that same dull aching discomfort I did near the Anne Frank House, only stronger.

Months later, I surrendered to the brutal Dutch winter. I was no longer able to withstand the freezing Arctic air and discomfort of living in a poorly insulated houseboat. River life sounded romantic, and it was, but only during the summer months. I met a local Jewish girl at a folk music club who offered to rent me space in her home. Coco was the daughter of a concert violinist who had been captured by the Nazis in 1941. Hitler spared her father's life and forced him to entertain the Nazis with his violin. Coco was born a year after the war ended.

One morning over breakfast, she gave me a history lesson about the Dutch Resistance of WWII.

"Do you know the monument located in the middle of Dam Square?" she asked in her strong Dutch accent.

"Sure. I walked near there almost every morning on my way to get breakfast," I replied. I didn't want to try to explain to Coco why I hadn't actually entered Dam Square.

"The Nazis shot and killed twenty-two of us at that horrible place. Eighty thousand Jews were deported to German concentration camps. It was twenty-five years ago but we will never forget," Coco said.

I didn't know what to say, so I said nothing. It was one of those moments when words reach the heart. Nazis, murders in the center of town, people hiding, concentration camps...it was too much to wrap my head around. But this had been the life of this young Jewish girl. I realized how lucky I was and how much I had taken for granted living in America.

Something I felt internally influenced me to avoid certain places. Each location turned out to be a place where something evil had happened or where innocent life had been destroyed. I had absolutely no idea what it was that made me turn away from these areas. I wrote it off as some type of hypersensitivity. The truth is, I really didn't know how to explain it. But time and time again, it happened.

10

Voices of War

Clairaudience: the ability to perceive sounds beyond the reach of ordinary experience

I was nearly broke. Actually, I *was* broke. As inexpensive as living in Europe was in 1970, my money was gone. Most of the summer tourists had left the Netherlands by the end of September. I was one of the few Americans who remained in Amsterdam. The phrase, "I went broke in Europe" had an adventurous and romantic tone to it, but that mystique was far from the truth. It was a scary and lonely feeling. It was a wake-up call and a time that I will never forget.

I remember that cold afternoon in the Rembrantsplein section of Amsterdam. I was wearing my long, black, silver-buttoned overcoat I had purchased in a marine surplus store on Cape Cod in Massachusetts.

The frigid North Sea wind blew hard from the Arctic Circle. I held my last silver Dutch coin in my hand. I knew that this day would be a nodal point in my life. I had never run out of money in my life. I had been the twelve-year-old kid who always had a hundred dollars in his pocket from caddying at the local golf club.

I wanted to spend my last Dutch quarter on something that I'd remember forever. At that moment, I made a promise to myself that this would be the last time I'd ever go broke. I walked across the cobblestone street into a cheese store and grabbed a chocolate bar off the shelf. I gave the clerk my last twenty-five Dutch cents. Aptly, the chocolate bar was called Studentenhaver, which means "Student's

Heaven" in English. I took a bite and realized quickly that I was no longer a student and was definitely not in heaven. It was time to find a job. I was tired and had no place to go. One never knows how they will behave when they're down and out. Thank God not everyone has to go through that experience. For me, it was something that activated my very soul. Don't get me wrong, I was afraid, very afraid. How would I buy food? Where would I live? Those questions plagued me for hours, not days. I didn't fall prey to feelings of despair. Those thoughts were there inside me, but getting food and shelter immediately, trumped that fear.

All I had to depend upon was a limited ability to sing and play guitar. The next day, I made a collect call to America and invited Timmy and Danny, two friends from high school, to join me in an adventure to perform music across Europe. This became my plan on which to focus. I didn't dwell on being broke—my thoughts were about moving beyond my lack of money.

Soon, the three of us, as Black River and Western, were playing four days a week and making money in clubs throughout the Netherlands. American music was well received throughout Europe. During a rare weekend off in April of 1971, I loaded Timmy and Danny into my VW camper and we headed to Paris. We were booked to audition for a club on the famous Left Bank of Paris. We had never played in France and were excited about the possible opportunity to work in Paris.

Amsterdam to Paris was a three-hundred-mile drive. I took the highway route south through Brussels. The guys wanted to stop in a picturesque Belgium village that a friend had told us about, so I pulled off the highway and we stopped for dinner in the French-speaking part of Belgium. Dinner lasted much longer than we anticipated. It was a rare night when we didn't have to be onstage, so we relaxed and enjoyed ourselves over food and wine.

"It's getting late, and we have three more hours before we get to Paris. We have an audition tomorrow. We should look for a place to camp. I don't want us to be tired at the audition," I said. That night, we had consumed more French wine than we should have—Bordeaux wine had an excellent year in 1971.

So we headed out, but soon, the vote to stop for the evening was unanimous. I exited the highway south of Brussels to find a place to camp away from the city. (We didn't want to have to drive through Brussels the following morning in rush hour traffic.) We continued farther south from Brussels, exited a secondary road, and drove another twenty minutes until we reached a large open field that I pulled into and parked. It was very dark. The full moon forced a soft glow through the damp night air. The area showed no signs of civilization. I was confident that we had found a safe and quiet place to sleep for the night.

Quickly, the air temperature cooled, and a thick fog crawled in across the field. The moon crept higher into the night sky, revealing knee-high grass across the field. I figured I had parked on the edge of a large farm. I spread my blankets inside the VW while the guys set up the portable tent outside at the rear of the camper. We knew we occasionally had to camp when we were away from Amsterdam, so we were prepared. More often than not, the band was provided with a room by the club owner who we were working for, but we hadn't yet been offered a contract.

I was very excited about the audition and the opportunity to work in France. It was also my first trip to Paris and my twenty-sixth birthday. April in Paris and a birthday celebration on The Rive Gauche...not too bad for a guy who had recently spent his last quarter on a candy bar!

As the fog thickened, it crept along the ground and shifted slowly back and forth like white ocean waves glowing in the moonlight. It was almost 1:00 a.m., so we didn't waste much time getting to sleep. The commonly held belief that musicians party every night was just a fantasy. The three of us were friends, but first and foremost, we were partners on a business trip.

About 3:00 a.m., I was awakened abruptly by the sound of men's voices. I remember wondering why Timmy and Danny were awake and talking in the middle of the night. Angry, I sat up in my camper bed and looked out the rear window. I saw that both of them were still asleep in their tent, but the voices continued. I finally realized they sounded far away, across the field. I wondered if it might be the police. *Maybe I parked on private property*, I thought. This wouldn't have been the first time the police had asked us to leave private property in the middle of the night. My sleepy curiosity got the best of me, so I pushed open the rear door of the camper and jumped outside to look around the field. No one was there.

Cold wet fog crept over my bare feet. I continued looking out across the field. Each anxious breath turned white and disappeared into the fog. Eventually, I crawled back under my blanket. *I must have heard an echo from a house far away*, I thought as I fell back asleep.

Suddenly, I woke again to the same sound of distant voices. It was 4:00 a.m. I cringed at the thought of a sleepless night. I propped my head up on the pillow and again, looked out the rear window. The sensation I experienced was unforgettable. This time, I heard the voices of hundreds of people on the fog-covered field, but *no one was there*. Male voices became more distinct. I couldn't understand any specific words. Between the voices, I heard yelling and screaming. Nothing made sense. I must have fallen back asleep at some point because at 7:00 a.m. there was a knock on the back of my camper. The guys were ready to get going. We shared some bread and Dutch cheese before continuing our drive south to Paris.

As the morning sun brightened the dew-covered field, I could see that we had indeed been parked in a very isolated area. There were no houses or towns in any direction. On the way back to the highway we saw a sign that read "Bataille de Waterloo." None of us spoke French but we figured that we had just camped out on the Waterloo Battlefield where Napoleon Bonaparte had met his defeat.

I didn't tell either of the guys about what I had heard that night. I wouldn't have known how to begin, plus I didn't want to have to deal with their comments and jokes for the next three hours. I had too much on my mind with our audition that afternoon, not to mention celebrating my twenty-sixth birthday in Paris.

At the time, it didn't occur to me that I might have had a clairaudient psychic experience that night on the Waterloo Battlefield. I really didn't know *what* had happened. I absolutely believed that my experience was real. I wasn't asleep or dreaming—it kept me awake half the night! As always, I felt then that it was in my own best interest not to think too much about these things. After all, I had become an expert in avoidance, and I didn't want to spoil my birthday by trying to understand what had happened that night. The fact was I *didn't understand* what had happened. Despite my best intentions, I did wonder if an event from the past could have been somehow imprinted upon the present, but I felt it became a waste of my time because I couldn't come up with any reasonable answer.

11

Dachau Memory

Clairsentience: the ability to feel physical and emotional states
of people and outside areas

Our band was booked to audition for the US Army in Heidelberg, Germany. We were scheduled to open for Ben E. King, the international recording star of "Stand by Me" and "Spanish Harlem" fame. We had been feeling sorry for ourselves having not been hired in Paris. The Paris club owner had been more interested in a jazz sound—we definitely did not meet his expectations. And so, this opportunity in Germany cheered us up immensely.

Everything was right with the world. Our practice and hard work had finally paid off. The Armed Forces Entertainment Special Services Group hired musical acts for military bases throughout Germany. This was a big deal. A producer at EMI Records in Holland believed that Black River and Western would be well received and probably be offered a long-term contract with the military. We were excited about the opportunity but a little cautious about becoming Army employees due to our shoulder-length hair.

That evening, we were the first act on stage. "Let's welcome, from the United States, Black River and Western!" the announcer boomed over the loudspeaker. The audience was filled with uniformed soldiers and civilians. Many were also booking agents from military bases throughout southern Germany. We sang a medley of songs to showcase our music and vocal harmonies. Their round of applause was something I'll never forget. The record producer in Holland had been correct—the audience loved us. They cheered. We were shocked and surprised.

We knew we were pretty good, but this was an over-the-top round of applause. Booking agents rushed the stage before we had a chance to put our instruments back into their cases. We actually signed our first contract before we left the stage. I was about to make more money than I had brought to Europe with me over a year ago.

"I heard that musicians receive 'officer privileges' when they're working on military bases," I said.

"I'm not sure about the details. But I was told that we'd be eating steak and lobster every night in the private Officer's Club," Timmy said, smiling.

I didn't immediately grasp the importance of "officer privilege" but learned that it allowed us to dine nightly in a private club—for almost nothing. Our contract insured that we'd play four shows a week at Army and Air Force bases in southern Germany. And the best part: we were to be paid daily.

Bavaria was more picturesque than northern Germany. But it was difficult to overlook the lingering evidence of the WWII allied bombing as we drove across southern Germany. Many times, we endured angry stares and insults from women who had lost their husbands during the war. The emotional wounds were most evident in the towns that were almost totally destroyed by allied bombing. An end to war does not always signal the beginning of peace. The residue of war continued to engulf the countryside with sadness. You could feel it in the air.

A week later, we were invited to play live on a radio show in Furth, a small town north of Munich. We got an early morning start on our drive to the radio station—we had an interview with the disc jockey at noon. He spoke to us in English then translated our comments into German for the listening audience. The interview was a great promotion for the club dates we had lined up in Munich. Following our interview, we sang one song before beginning our return to Munich. About halfway back, we saw a road sign for Dachau.

"Let's go take a look at that place," Danny said. His father had been an American prisoner of war in Germany. Though his dad had never been held in a concentration camp, Danny was still interested in the idea of visiting one. I reluctantly agreed to take the detour to

Dachau. I thought to myself that a visit to a concentration camp was a crazy waste of time—I was not in the mood for it but relented.

"I don't see any street signs," I shouted in frustration as we drove around. "This is not one of your popular tourist attractions, so why are we going?"

We stopped to ask for directions, but no one would speak to us. It was not a language difficulty...they just didn't want to talk to Americans. Some people waved their arms and pointed vaguely, while others just walked away. It was clear they had not forgotten the war.

It became more and more evident that the local people viewed the concentration camp as a "bad dream" that they couldn't wake up from. Most were puzzled why we wanted to visit there in the first place. In the minds of the locals, Dachau did not exist. In 1971, there were no tour buses headed to Dachau. Things got even more surreal when we passed the Dachau Golf Club.

"The Germans built a private country club near the concentration camp? Something is just not right about that," I said. I began to feel restless when we were less than a mile from the entrance to the camp.

The day was damp and overcast. My VW camper was the only vehicle on the narrow street. I drove slowly past some old wooden buildings. They looked like dormitories that had likely housed Nazi guards. Farther along the road, I saw long narrow buildings in ruins. The tile floors were still intact. One building looked like a stable. *Probably where the Nazi SS kept their horses,* I thought. I stopped in front of a tall iron entrance gate.

"I don't want to go in. I don't feel good. I'll wait out here. You guys take your time," I said.

"Okay. You sure? We'll be inside if you change your mind," someone said.

A strong physical sensation gripped my stomach area. I began to feel ill and angry at the same time. My body shook like I was cold... but it wasn't that cold. Something seemed to be taking hold of me... something unpleasant. It made me feel squirmy. I considered driving away from the area but was afraid I'd get lost due to the lack of street signs. I calmed myself down and grabbed the Michelin road map to figure out exactly where I was parked. I figured that if I kept my mind active studying the map, I might feel better. A distinct energy sensation surrounded my upper body. It reminded me of the negative energy I had felt in Amsterdam. The energy pushed at me. I tried to nap but couldn't. I kept thinking about Amsterdam and what had happened when I walked near the Anne Frank House and Dam Square.

I knew not to go inside this concentration camp. The strong sensation had given me the clear message to stay away. I sat in my camper bus at the main gate for over an hour. My mind drifted. I suddenly remembered what Mada Love had said years earlier. She told everyone that we had been reincarnated from souls who died in WWII. She never actually explained how we died. Ringo had saluted me that day, as if we had been soldiers. I struggled with the alternative explanation as I stared at the large iron entrance gate to the Dachau gas chamber. I considered the possibility that Mada was referring to a different kind of death—one so terrible that it was unspeakable...a death here at Dachau. *This is crazy*, I thought. *I'm getting carried away with crazy possibilities*. Or was I?

12

I Saw the Dead Soldier

Clairvoyance: it can often be like watching a movie in your head

I met Koholo the night we played the Rathskeller Club (The Club) in Idar-Oberstein Germany. Forty-eight hours earlier, he had been fighting on the front lines in Vietnam. Ko was Hawaiian. Unexpectedly, that same night, I also met Ko's brother—I'll try to explain.

Idar-Oberstein is a picturesque village situated on a tributary of the Rhine River. Driving into the village reminded me of a photo in a travel brochure. Despite its quaint appearance, it was not your typical tourist town. The idyllic setting hid the fact that twenty-five years earlier, the village served as a major garrison for the Nazi Third Reich. When we were there, the US Army used the base as a reintegration center for American GIs. It was a stopover point for soldiers returning from the front lines of Vietnam. Idar-Oberstein was the quiet village where battle-weary GIs could relax and readjust before returning "back to the world," as the GIs referred to America. We were booked to play in The Club for a week. We too needed some readjustment to a military base.

Ko was a short, dark-haired young man a few years younger than I was. He was eager to talk with a fellow American about everything he had missed out on. His questions focused on current events, sports, and music. Soldiers on the front line were cut off from almost everything back home. Ko had been out of touch in Vietnam for quite some time.

"Are you finished with your tour of duty?" I asked.

"I have to go home," he said, and paused. "My brother was killed by the Viet Cong. I'm the only male left in my family. The Army is sending me back to Hawaii so I can take care of my mother," he said sadly.

Hesitantly at first, Ko began to talk about his brother. It was apparent that his brother's death had not completely registered with him. I sat at a table during the band's break and listened while he reminisced about the two of them growing up in Hawaii, years before it became a state.

As he spoke, I felt an electric serenity overcome me. This energetic chill surrounded my shoulders. As I listened to Ko's words, my attention was drawn away from our conversation and into a jungle environment in my mind's eye. *But Ko is talking about Hawaii, not a jungle*, I thought to myself. As he spoke, I watched a movie play out in my mind about something quite different. My vision had nothing to do with Ko's stories of his childhood,

I had a *vision* of war. I *saw* in my mind's eye a young man being killed in a flash of orange fire. My attention shifted. Ko's voice was left behind and I was somewhere else. I was in a place between Ko and a jungle. I saw a person who resembled Ko. The image lasted a few moments. I felt terror and fear. It was as if I were in the jungle with other men. They were being burned to death. I felt *inside* the experience of my vision. I was with Ko's brother when he died.

Moments later, my focus returned to Ko. He was still talking about Hawaii in the old days. The vision had been brief, but quite intense. Even today, fifty years later, the experience remains fixed in my memory. At the time, I thought that this was the result of my having a vivid imagination. I wanted to forget about what had just happened and blame it on my imagination. After all, I was on a band break and had to get back on stage.

Years later, I accepted that that experience was an early exposure to mediumship. Energetically, the spirit of the deceased soldier moved into my clairvoyant vision. For a brief moment, Ko's brother's spirit allowed me to know the terror of war.

13

THE PROOF IS IN YOUR PALM

Palmistry: a psychic practice thought to have begun in India 3000 years ago

—S. Dwivedi, 1970

Saint Nicolas Eve is a very special day in the Netherlands. Santa Claus rides down the streets of Amsterdam on a white horse while his elves hand out gifts to all the children waiting eagerly along Damrak street. It's every kid's Christmas fantasy: a face-to-face meeting with Santa. My head was flooded with childhood memories, and I wanted nothing more than to be a kid again on that cobblestone street, waiting for my Christmas present from Santa.

I had been working five to six nights a week, back and forth between the Netherlands and Germany. The weekly commute between Amsterdam and Hamburg was tiresome, to say the least. I needed a break. One evening, I picked up Timmy and Danny and drove across town to the Jordaan section of Amsterdam. The Jordaan neighborhood had been home to Rembrandt and for that reason, was normally much too expensive for a night out on the town. But now I was a working musician with a job and money in my pocket. Going to dinner in the Jordaan neighborhood would feel like a personal triumph...a little reminder that we had made it—for the time being anyway. It hadn't been all that long since I had spent my last Dutch quarter on a chocolate candy bar.

Around 11:00 p.m., after we'd finished our expensive meals, an attractive young woman with long dark hair walked into the restaurant. She was alone.

"What do you suppose she's up to?" Danny asked.

"This restaurant is too high-class to allow a 'woman of the night' in here," Timmy said. We watched while the young woman stopped for a moment at each table. Finally, she reached our table and, surprisingly, sat down with the three of us. We froze.

"Would you like me to read your palm?" she asked in a soft Spanish accent. My negative reply was lost beneath the others' enthusiasm. I was more than ready to call it a night and get back to my apartment.

"Sure. You can read my palm," Danny said eagerly.

I barely listened as the woman read the palms of my bandmates. She repeated common catch phrases about the health and happiness each had enjoyed in their lives. She briefly got my attention when she told one of them that he was a musician and would work as a musician for the rest of his life. I figured that the woman was a good guesser. After all, it would not have been too far a reach to assume that we were all musicians. Our hair was longer than anyone else's in the restaurant, and we were Americans. (By the way, that palm reader was absolutely correct. In fact, as far as I am aware, both Danny and Timmy still work as musicians.) Once she had finished reading their palms, I motioned to the others that it was time to leave.

"We already paid for your palm reading," they reminded me.

I was reluctant but decided to get it over with. I realized that this woman was no different than the three of us. She was from another country and reading palms to support herself. We were all ex-patriots just trying to make a living.

"All right," I said holding out both of my hands.

The woman took my hands into hers. She studied one, then the other. Her index finger occasionally touched along the lines of my outstretched palm. She didn't speak for what seemed like minutes. I sat quietly while the others looked on.

"The lines of your left palm show me the gift God bestowed upon you," she said when she finally spoke. I looked over at the others who had just ordered another round of Heinekens. I knew we weren't leaving anytime soon.

"Your right hand tells me what you are doing with the gift that God has given you in this life," she continued. Up to this point, the woman hadn't mentioned a thing related to health or happiness as she had with the others.

"You have the Mystic Cross between your head, heart, and life lines of both your left and right palms. You have a predisposition for Spirit and the supernatural world," she continued. My two partners drew closer as the woman pointed to the lines on my palms. I had little to no understanding of anything she was saying to me.

"You have a seven-pointed star on the heart line of your left hand," she said while touching the center of my hand. "See the triangle at the end of the Line of Fate on your right hand?" she pointed. "You were psychic in your past lifetime, and you are psychic now in this lifetime," she said as she stood up.

"That's cool," Timmy remarked.

"Yeah, a cool waste of money. Let's go home," I said.

I thought the woman was just trying to end our session with a dramatic flair. A big-bang finish was maybe her way of getting a bigger tip. It was interesting, but I had no intention of getting a turban or a crystal ball. I didn't pay much attention to what she had said. It was fun, but nothing more than that.

Eleven years later, I would hear very similar words from another psychic in Boston.

14

SPOOKY LONDON

Synchronicity: meaningful coincidence of two or
more events where something other than the probability
of chance is involved

—Carl Jung, 1951

Drugs had become rampant in Amsterdam. By 1972, the first Cannabis Cafe had opened. Marijuana, cocaine, and heroin were everywhere. Unfortunately, after this news got around, many of Europe's drug addicts moved to Amsterdam. One afternoon, I opened the door of the neighborhood phone booth and was shocked by a young guy shooting heroin into his left arm. He was kneeling at the bottom of the booth—probably so he wouldn't have far to fall in case he overdosed. I slammed the phone booth door before he had a chance to say anything. I'm not even sure he would have been coherent. It felt like I was watching someone commit a slow suicide.

It shook me to the core. I had never seen someone with a needle hanging in their arm before. In that moment, I knew that it was time to get myself out of the Netherlands. My happy feeling of being on a European vacation had vanished. I was burned out.

I saw an ad in the *International Herald Tribune* that a new American School had opened on the east coast of England. Having briefly taught biology, chemistry, and physics in America, I figured I could find some work at the school within one of those subject areas—I was a science triple threat. Perhaps a life in England could be a way to recover from my burnout.

The Birth of an American Medium

I arrived at The American School in England early in 1972. On my first weekend, I piled Joanne, Jean, and Will—a few fellow faculty members—into my VW camper for an excursion into London.

I parked near Hyde Park so we could explore the South Kensington neighborhood. On the way there, one of the faculty members pointed to a Free Admission sign on the door of a large nineteenth century Victorian building—just what we needed to see since we were still weeks away from our first payday at The American School.

Inside the building, we entered a room with large glass cabinets that stood along the walls. The ancient oak floor squeaked every time I took a step and there was a musty smell as if no one had been inside for years. A donation box sat on top of the desk, next to a pile of brochures for The Society of Psychical Research.

"What is this place?" I asked.

"There's photographs of ghosts in these cabinets," Jean, who taught history, replied.

I moved to the glass cabinet to look more closely at the photographs. They were dark and grainy. One showed a man with a strange white substance that looked like cotton candy drifting out of his mouth. Another showed a similar substance forming into a "ghost-like" individual. Each of the glass cabinets had exhibits of ghost photos. Some of the pictures looked extremely old, others were more recent.

"I've never seen anything like this before," I said.

"Look at the famous names on that wall plaque. Sigmund Freud, William James, Carl Jung, Arthur Conan Doyle—they were all members of this Society," Joanne, the English teacher, said.

I continued to study the photos in each of the display cases. The small print at the bottom of one the photographs read, "This is a substantiated photo showing a physical medium and ectoplasm."

This is bizarre, I thought. I was a science teacher yet had never heard of "supernatural ectoplasm." I was stunned and amazed. In all my years as a student of science, I had never heard of this phenomenon. I picked up one of the brochures and began to read. It explained that since 1882, England had been the educational center for the study of mediumship. I hadn't heard the word "medium" since my visit to the mountains of North Georgia three years earlier. I had discovered a new world. I wasn't sure if I believed my eyes. It was a bit like learning that life existed on another planet. I didn't know if this was real, or a hoax. The one name that stuck with me that day was Gordon Higginson.

I don't believe in coincidence. Wandering into that building in 1972 was a special moment for me. The British showed an acceptance and willingness to study a phenomenon that, to my knowledge, had never been openly discussed in America. That day served as a minor vindication for my view of reality. For years, I had wondered if there was something wrong with me. Why was I able to *see* and *feel* energy when most people were not? What purpose could it possibly serve? What exactly was a medium? Now, I had found photos and a Society that was devoted to finding answers. That day, I breathed a little easier.

The day I visited the Society of Psychical Research in 1972 was a synchronicity. And the same can be said, when in 2015, I received mediumship training from Mavis Pittilla, who had been taught by the man pictured in the brochure that day, Mr. Gordon Higginson.

15

THE BOSTON TEA ROOM PSYCHIC

Psychic: a person sensitive to forces believed to come
from beyond the natural world

My career flourished. Teaching school in England eventually led to a headmaster position at an American School in the Canary Islands. To this day, I have to smile, trying to figure how in one year I went from traveling Europe in a folk-rock band to becoming the headmaster of a private international school in the Canary Islands. Life had put me in the right place at the right time.

The Canaries, located off the coast of western Africa, was an island paradise. It sounds like an exciting adventure, and it was. But I was turning thirty and felt like I had not yet settled down. The relationship with my girlfriend had fallen apart and I began to miss my parents and siblings. I wasn't getting any younger. I felt lonely and *was* totally alone. Whenever I had experienced burnout, I tried to make something positive happen by getting active. After much thought, I decided to travel to Boston to continue with graduate education. Education became my focus and my new plan. If I ever wanted to return to Europe and work in a great school in Paris or London, it was going to take my earning a doctorate degree.

I was accepted into the summer program at Harvard. I guess my career track from traveling rock band to headmaster piqued their interest. Having had experience as an administrative leader in an international school at a very young age had taught me a great lesson—on a very primitive level—that I didn't know a thing about being a leader or a manager. Harvard gave me the opportunity to study budgetary analysis and human behavior, two important components of management.

I had a week free before classes began. One afternoon in Cambridge, I received a call from my friend, ironically named Yale, who wanted to introduce me to some of Boston's historical sites. I had met Yale during the time I was a headmaster in the Canary Islands.

Though I was born in Boston, I didn't know very much about the city because, as mentioned earlier, we'd moved to Connecticut. We agreed to be true tourists for the day and take a walking tour of the city. Our route began on Tremont Street.

"Let's stop for coffee first," I suggested.

"How about tea? There's a place up the street that might remind you of Europe," Yale said. We walked down Tremont Street and stopped in front of a sign that read, Boston Tea Room.

"It's up there, on the sixth floor," Yale pointed.

We walked up the six flights and entered a large open room filled with small round tables covered with white lace tablecloths. The shades were drawn on the row of windows that faced Tremont Street. The strong aroma of tea hung in the air. I was still scanning the room for an empty table when a woman approached.

"Are you here for a psychic reading or just tea?"

"Both." Yale smiled.

"Please be seated on the bench. A table will open soon," the woman said. We sat quietly. Eventually, the woman placed an old silver teapot and two China cups in front of us.

"This place is pretty busy for a weekday afternoon," I said.

"It's a well-known spot. Don't forget, Boston is a major tourist town. Besides, a lot of people have an interest in hearing from a psychic," Yale said.

"Come on. Really?" I replied.

We kept refilling our teacups. Every few minutes, we glanced toward the tables, looking for an available psychic, but every table remained occupied. About a half-hour later, we were waved over to an open table.

"You go first," I said.

"No. No, this is for you. I've already gone through this initiation," Yale said.

I headed to the far end of the room and sat down in a chair opposite a woman who looked to be in her late twenties. I had expected someone much older. My immediate thought was that she looked much too young to be a psychic. She looked nothing like the woman in the purple turban that I saw in Manhattan when I was a kid. Her white shirt and fitted skirt made her look more like a Boston executive on her lunch break than a tearoom psychic. Nervously, I ran my fingers along the embroidered edge of the lace tablecloth. I was uncomfortable with the whole process and became even more uncomfortable when she took my hand into hers.

"Your friend across the state line is in much trouble," the woman quickly began. I thought to myself, *what is she talking about?*

"No. No, I don't know what that means," I said. The woman didn't respond. She was staring past me in a kind of daze. She showed little interest in my negative response.

"You drive a very funny little car," she said.

"I have a little green VW. But I don't know about 'funny,' " I replied.

The woman continued. Her eyes closed. I quietly waited for the ordeal to be over. My friend had mentioned that the psychic usually provided three pieces of information before the reading was finished. *She already has two strikes against her,* I thought.

"You are psychic. No?" she asked rhetorically. At that point, she opened her eyes and looked directly at me.

"No," I replied almost defensively.

The woman smiled at me then looked away. My reading was finished. Thank God! There was no further discussion. I stood up, returned to where Yale was waiting, and we left immediately, continuing our walk toward Beacon Hill.

"So? What did she say?" he asked.

"She said I have a 'funny little car.' I told her it wasn't true." Yale laughed.

"What's so funny?" I asked.

"You drive a ten-year-old Volkswagen Beetle. The green paint has worn down to the steel. Both of the running boards have fallen off and there's a hole in the floor on the passenger side. Jim, when I look down, I can see the road when you're driving me around Boston! You don't think that falls into the 'funny' category?" Yale asked.

"I guess so," I said reluctantly. "She also told me that 'my friend across the state line was in trouble.' That statement was a clear miss."

About six months later, I got a call at my apartment in Cambridge that Emily, a woman I had known in Europe, had suffered an emotional breakdown and had been hospitalized the same week I received the psychic reading at the Boston Tea Room.

I never mentioned to Yale what the woman had said about my being psychic. I'm not sure why. I guess I was always doing my best to avoid that part of myself. I couldn't shake the image of turbans and crystal balls in the basement rooms of Times Square.

16

THE HARVARD ASTROLOGER

"Much later in your life, something will happen, and you will once again use your psychic gifts."

—Rick, Harvard astrologer, 1977

Harvard College was the last place you'd think to look for an astrologer. However, I found Cambridge to be filled with interesting people with many talents. Their talents were not necessarily those that got them into Harvard in the first place. A few weeks before classes began, our friend David, Yale, and I stopped by the apartment of his friend, Rick, who had recently returned to Harvard from his summer break. Rick was a math and astronomy major but had a vast knowledge and understanding of astrology.

David, who hosted a cable TV show on astrology at the time, led the way up to Rick's second-floor apartment. Suddenly, we were in the presence of two semi-famous Boston astrologers. They began discussing a new book written by their astrology teacher, Isabel Hickey—in fact, I believe David went on to become one of her protégés. The idea that Rick, a Harvard astronomy student, was also studying astrology got my attention.

The walls and ceiling of Rick's apartment were covered with a heavy, shiny, linen-like paper, similar to that used to wrap sandwiches at the off-campus Jewish deli. The eight planets of the solar system were painted in vibrant colors across the walls and ceiling. Superimposed onto the solar system drawings were paper cutouts of each planet, showing their daily transit positions in the solar system. I had never seen anything like it before.

"You must have a very understanding landlord," I joked.

"Would you like me to arrange the planets to their exact location on the day you were born?" Rick asked.

"Sure. Why not?" I replied.

While one astrologer consulted his ephemeris book, the other arranged the planets to their solar position on the day of my birth. They then began to interpret my astrology chart, describing both past and present events. I was astounded by their accuracy to note specific dates when I had moved from country to country. Most amazing was Rick's description of my personality traits. The information appeared to be based on science, or at least some version of science. Before finishing, they consulted about an aspect in my chart involving the planet Neptune and its angle to the moon.

"I don't know whether or not you believe in reincarnation, but you have an aspect here that leads me to believe that you were psychic in your last incarnation," Rick said. My friends looked on with interest. I had never mentioned to anyone that a medium in North Georgia, a palm reader in Amsterdam, and a psychic at the Boston Tea Room had all made the exact same statement to me. This was now the fourth time I'd been told. I was nervously confused.

"I may have heard that before," I said hesitantly.

"Well, the placement of this aspect suggests that you were psychic during your past life," Rick said emphatically. He paused for a moment, pointed to Neptune, and commented about how it formed a square to my Saturn and my vertex in the eighth house…the house representing death. I was beginning to get a little scared. I didn't know what any of this stuff meant. Every time someone tried to tell me about being psychic, it only upset me. Things aren't fun when you don't understand them. Besides, I was in Cambridge to continue my education, not to start a new life as a psychic.

Rick continued on to say that Neptune was a very important planet in my astrology chart. It was connected to other planets at specific angles found only in the astrology charts of psychics and mediums. I listened and tried to comprehend what he was saying, but really didn't want to.

"You didn't always use your psychic gift with the best intention," Rick said.

What the hell does that mean? This is only getting worse, I said to myself.

"Much later in your life, something will happen, and you will once again use your psychic gifts," Rick said firmly.

I didn't say a word. Rick stared at me, a serious look on his face. He was a no-nonsense type of fellow. I didn't know what to make of all his talk about astrology, past lives, and psychic gifts. He was a seemingly intelligent Harvard student, talking to me about being psychic. It was not exactly what I had expected to hear that afternoon and it was all too strange to wrap my mind around. For a minute, I thought he was trying to scare me with his explanation about being "psychic in a past life" and "not always using my gift with the best intention." Leaving the apartment, I couldn't get his final words out of my head. *Much later in your life, something will happen, and you will once again use your psychic gifts.*

He told me to stop by his apartment anytime. I never did.

That afternoon in Cambridge, Massachusetts had a paradoxical effect upon me. Everything I had been told was too far-fetched for me to handle. And, even if it were true, I didn't want to waste time at that point in my life. The summer in Cambridge had provided me with the knowledge and confidence that I could one day earn a doctorate degree. My classmates had awarded me first place for my summer project on the budgetary analysis of not-for-profit organizations. Though this sounds like part of a business program, it was actually an important part of my studies in organizational psychology. The following year, I learned that my photo was in the Harvard summer course catalogue. I suppose it was a parting gift from my professor for having done well in class. Later that fall, I would leave Cambridge and finally return home for employment and many years of graduate school and doctoral research at a university in Connecticut. Hard work was my new reality, not the psychic world.

17

THE PSYCHIC PSYCHOLOGIST

"There was a cognitive dissonance between the words I was hearing and the energy I was feeling."

—J. Deary, 1983

One morning in the fall of 1983, I had an experience that convinced me not to work directly with patients in a clinical setting. While completing my counseling psychology practicum, I was conducting psychotherapy sessions with patients, under the supervision of my professor.

One evening, I had a session with a young married couple. The wife initiated the session. She and her husband began by reviewing a long list of problem areas in their lives. The wife insisted that it was her husband who needed counseling help, not her. She labeled him as the "problem person." Their issues were not unlike those of many young newlyweds.

I listened intently to them as they spoke. I was focused and had an open mind. (I had learned never to jump to conclusions.) As they continued to politely describe things from their perspectives, I felt an energy sensation in my stomach. I somehow *knew* that it was the wife who needed my help and not the husband. I felt her sense of urgency although that urgency was not supported by her words or behavior. The husband's anxiety was palpable but this knowingness continued to focus my attention on the wife. I knew she was having extreme emotional difficulties despite her calm and reserved persona.

One does not have to be trained in counseling psychology to suspect that in many cases both the husband and wife share the responsibility for events that occur in their marriage. However, this internal feeling continued to overwhelm me. I felt that the wife was in trouble. My experience with the two of them that evening confused me. There was a cognitive dissonance between the words I was hearing and the energy I was feeling.

The source of this energy was very similar to the energy information that I had received in my parents' living room when I was a kid, watching Jimmy Murphy tell the story of when he bit his horse. Here I was, conducting a clinical family therapy session with a married couple and receiving some sixth sense information. I didn't like what was happening. It was confusing and more importantly, did not seem professional. Was this what I had to look forward to every time I had a patient sitting in front of me?

Similar experiences happened on a few more occasions. I was not at all happy. My confusion caused me to question my career choice. I still had time to make a slight career detour. I decided to focus my doctoral research in the area of group decision-making and organizational development. My research study would therefore be less clinical and more of a study in management psychology. My new career goal was to work as a behavioral scientist within a clinical healthcare environment.

Months later, I learned from a colleague who had taken over the couple's therapy case that the wife had been involved in an extramarital affair throughout her therapy. While I have met psychologists and psychiatrists who claim to be able to incorporate the psychic information they receive into their therapeutic models, I was not. For me, these are two very different approaches to working with the human psyche. Psychology utilizes a cognitive approach, while using psychic methods is an energetic approach. It was impossible for me to stay focused on the patient while the energy of feeling and knowing flooded my awareness. I knew I had a professional problem with the mechanism of incorporating both models into the clinical setting. Looking back, I believe I made the correct career decision.

18

Pizza Synchronicity

"If you follow the path, your life will totally change."

—The Perfect Stranger, 1984

Friday night was pizza night. I usually stopped for take-out on my drive home from Manhattan to Connecticut. In 1984, my partners and I were in the early stages of developing a health care organization in New York City. The workdays were long and Friday night was my time to relax at home.

One particular Friday, there was an extra-long wait for take-out, so I went next door into the bookstore to kill some time. Inside, I was drawn to a woman who was looking at a book in the New Age section. She was well-dressed, in her seventies, and had grey hair and penetrating blue eyes. As I approached her, I could see she was reading an astrology book written by Isabel Hickey—the teacher of the Harvard astrologer (Rick) who had given me an astrology reading in his Cambridge apartment years earlier.

She looked up at me and smiled. I'm essentially a shy person and usually the last person to initiate a conversation with anyone... but this time I did.

"I see you're reading Isabel's book. She's a great astrologer. I knew some of her students in Cambridge at Harvard," I said. The woman looked at me in surprise.

"Isabel was my best friend. She passed away five years ago," she said.

"Oh no! I'm so sorry. I hadn't heard. Two of her students once told me that I had psychic ability," I blurted out.

For reasons I couldn't comprehend, I opened up to her as if I'd known her all my life. I told her that Rick had said "something would happen to me later in my life" that would allow me to use my psychic abilities. I told her they said I was a psychic in my past life. It was like a confession that I knew she would understand. I told her things that I had never shared with anyone.

"I'm a psychic," the woman interrupted.

Oh my God, I thought. *It's happening again? I can't go anywhere without running into psychics!*

I was surprised, but at the same time, had almost expected that this stranger was a psychic. After all, I had initiated the conversation with her. I felt comfortable with her right from the time I met her. Technically, I never did "meet" her—we never actually introduced ourselves—I never asked her name, nor did she ask mine. This was another in a long line of synchronous events that I had experienced. I believe that our chance meeting was Spirit saying to me, "we know you're here, we know who you are, we know where you're going," and "everything is okay."

"Let me have a look at your left hand," the woman said.

As I opened my left hand and offered it to her, she took a pink crystal attached to the end of a gold chain from her pocketbook. She held it about three inches above my palm. Within seconds, the pink stone began to spin rapidly in a circle. It defied gravity. She was not moving her hand, yet the crystal spun faster and faster above my palm. It lasted for about twenty or thirty seconds until she moved it away.

"If you follow 'the path' your life will totally change," she said.

I didn't have to ask. I knew what she meant. If I followed the path of a psychic, my life would totally change. *But*, I thought, *I don't want my life to totally change*. Things were going pretty well the way they were.

"You know, you are able to talk to Isabel anytime you want," the woman continued.

As she was leaving the bookstore, she removed a photo of an angel from her pocketbook and handed it to me.

"Keep this angel with you," she said.

I thanked her and headed next door to get my pizza. That night, I tried to make sense of my brief meeting with her. I had opened up to a perfect stranger about things I had never mentioned to anyone ever before. I looked at the palm of my left hand and remembered the palm reader in Amsterdam in 1971. She had pointed to the seven-pointed star and triangles on my left palm. She had used the word "psychic."

And what did this woman mean when she said that I could "talk to Isabel anytime I want?" Isabel was dead. How was I supposed to talk to a dead person?

Although I went to that pizza place many Friday nights over the years, I never saw her again. As I didn't get her name, I could not search for her.

More than thirty years later, I still carry that photo of the angel with me every day. This woman was, in many ways, the perfect stranger.

As was foretold by the astrologer in Cambridge, something strange did begin to happen to me when I got older. Despite my best efforts to forget all about what the psychics, palm readers, and astrologers had been telling me, I couldn't. It was like another world wanted my undivided attention. While I was becoming very successful in New York City, more and more supernatural events were getting my attention. I couldn't explain them to myself, so I didn't try. I felt alone and isolated—like I was living in two worlds. As expert as I had become in my ability to avoid all things psychic, it was becoming more and more difficult to do so.

One weekend in 1992, I drove up to Vermont with my friend, Tammy. I had reservations at one of those idyllic inns that are often depicted in New England travel brochures. It was a beautiful fall weekend, trees in full colorful splendor, and getting away from the traffic and crowds of Manhattan was a welcomed treat. When we arrived, I parked in the lot behind the inn and took our bags out of the trunk. Intense sunshine illuminated the red and yellow leaves surrounding the property, making it look as if it were glowing. As I walked across the parking lot, I looked up at the historic New England inn towering above the oak and maple trees.

In an instant, I was overcome by a frightening vision. The inn was on fire! Orange flames engulfed the roof above the third floor.

Flames shot at least fifty feet up into the sky. The fire was consuming the middle section of the inn. The vision lasted three or four seconds. I froze mid-step, releasing the suitcases onto the pavement with a thud.

"What's the matter?" Tammy asked. Again, up to this point, I hadn't said much to anyone regarding my paranormal experiences.

"I just *saw* the inn burning. It—it—it was on fire," I stuttered.

"What? What are you talking about?" she asked.

"I'm not sure we should be staying here," I replied.

Still stunned, I picked up the suitcases and continued into the hotel lobby. My body was shaking. I was reacting as if I had really witnessed a fire. I wondered if I had just had a psychic premonition about a fire yet to happen.

I became really scared. Reluctantly, I checked us into the hotel. The desk clerk said our room would be ready in a half hour. We walked around the lobby area and into the tavern adjacent to the two-hundred-year-old inn.

"Come over here! Look! You won't believe this!" Tammy yelled.

She was pointing at a photograph on the wall that connected the inn with the tavern. The black and white photo showed the inn engulfed in flames. Fire shot up through the third-floor roof, just as I had seen in my vision. I was speechless, yet relieved. *At least the fire was in the past and not the future.* I breathed a sigh of relief, knowing that the inn would hopefully not catch fire while we slept.

Then confusion took over. The photo on the wall was one hundred percent *exactly as I had seen* in my vision. I had never been to the inn before in my life. There was no way that the memory of this fire had been locked away in my mind. We were two-hundred miles from home. *How was this possible? Was this some kind of energetic imprint? Is this what it means to be psychic?* I didn't want to get upset and frightened on a vacation weekend! *How can this ability be called a gift when all I'm left with is anxiety?*

A few months later, I was in Florida visiting my brother for the holidays. He had a few days off but was unexpectedly called back to his office at the Miami Branch of the Federal Bureau of Investigation. It had something to do with increased activity of the Colombian drug cartel in South Florida. I was alone for the day and due to rain, unable to play golf. So instead, I attended a workshop—in my hotel—on past lives, given by Dr. Brian Weiss, MD who was a respected psychiatrist from the Mt. Sinai School of Medicine in Manhattan. By then, I was a psychologist who had a professional curiosity regarding past lives. The possibility of past life had been suggested to me so many times by mediums, psychics, astrologers, and palm readers, that I figured that attending the workshop would be better than playing golf in the rain.

Dr. Weiss led the class through an exercise in relaxation. I felt like I had entered an altered state, similar to being hypnotized. He led us back in time to view our past lives. While in the relaxed state, I experienced being a Roman soldier, someone in Germany during WWII, an infantryman during the Civil War, and a religious priest in India. None of it made much sense. The exercise was interesting but there was no hard evidence that any of this had actually happened. The part about WWII and a religious priest struck a chord as it reflected what Mada Love had told me back in 1967 up in the mountains of North Georgia. *But,* my critical mind thought, *maybe that was just autosuggestion?* I needed hard evidence of past life...but at that time, there was none. I considered leaving at lunchtime, but the rain continued, so I stayed for the afternoon session.

After lunch, Dr. Weiss instructed us to pair up with the person to our left. He guided us through another relaxation exercise. The audience moaned when he told everyone to describe something about the person we were paired with. The class of nearly a hundred believed Dr. Weiss had given us an impossible task. No sooner did I say to myself, *This is crazy,* when a vision began to play out in my mind. Still in a super-relaxed state, I began to speak to the woman on my left.

"I see what looks like a vacation home. It's on a large lake. The house is big...like a place where rich people live. It's built with real logs made from trees. There's a large modern-looking glass window in the front. The window faces toward mountains," I said. The woman turned toward me, a dumfounded look on her face.

"Have we met before?" she asked.

"No. I don't think so. I'm from Connecticut. I'm here on vacation. Why?" I asked.

"You just described my family's house in the mountains of North Carolina. How did you do that?" she asked.

"I have no idea. It came to me like a movie in my head," I said.

That experience left me with a feeling of accomplishment, coupled with disbelief and fear. I did something that people aren't supposed to be able to do. And I didn't know how or why I was able to do it!

Until the age of fifty, I had never experienced the passing of a close loved one.

"Jimmy, take your brothers and sister and go get something to eat. I'll stay here with your father," Mom had said to us, just a few hours before Dad died in his hospital bed. My mother was there by his side, alone. She had wanted it that way, and so did he.

Two days later, my mother spoke to us about her final moments with Dad. The five of us sat in the living room, supporting one another. No one was saying much of anything when Mom broke the silence.

"Your father is in heaven, you know," she said. Knowing how difficult the last few weeks had been for Mom, the four of us just nodded in agreement.

"No, you don't understand," she continued. We turned toward her.

"I thought they were taking me along with him," she said. I could see by the look on Mom's face that she had experienced something that she wanted to talk about.

"I know you kids probably won't believe me, but after your father took his last breath, I saw a white light. Then, a burst of energy of some kind lifted me up out of my chair. I got scared and yelled. The nurse heard me and came running in. I was still rubbing my behind when she came in."

"What do mean?" my sister asked.

"I was dropped back down so hard on my chair that my behind was sore. I was almost thrown out of the chair," she said.

We sat there, amazed. I didn't say a thing. We didn't know whether to laugh or cry. Something profound had happened to our mother. I knew that Mom was able to see Spirit for as long as I could remember, although no one outside of the family ever knew about it. It was a closely held family secret. Later that day, she shared her experience with her parish priest. I'm not sure if he believed her or just thought she was a woman distraught over the death of her husband. I believed my mother because I too had seen something in the hospital room...something that I couldn't explain.

I didn't tell anyone in the family about the apparition I saw hours before my dad passed. Let's face it: in 1995, most people didn't accept the existence of paranormal events. There were no TV shows or movies about psychics. The words psychic and medium were hardly ever mentioned anywhere. If you saw anything spooky or strange, people either laughed at your expense or thought there was something very wrong with you.

That day, there were eight or nine bodily forms standing behind my father's bed. I don't want to call them angels, because I couldn't see them clearly. But after Dad passed, they were gone. Since that day, I've seen apparitions standing behind people who were about to pass. They seem to show up about a day before the person passes away, then, after the individual physically dies, they're gone. I've seen these visions on multiple occasions. Until now, I've always kept them to myself.

19

FEMALE HOUSE SPIRIT

"What happened here?"

—J. Deary, Connecticut, 2000

On Easter Sunday, I picked Mom up and drove her to my brother's house near the Connecticut River. It was my first visit to the small 18th century New England house where Tom lived with his girlfriend.

I walked hand in hand with my mother along the large stone steps leading up to a small foyer that separated the kitchen from the living room. As I entered the house, a strange weakness overtook both of my legs. I let go of mom's hand, and she continued down the hallway and into the living room. I stopped and reached for the wall to keep from falling. I felt my body being pushed *and* pulled down toward the floor. The sensation I felt was so strong that I nearly fell to my knees.

I yelled out, "What happened here?" I was startled by the volume of my own voice. I am usually quiet and reserved, not the type of guy who would walk into a house on Easter Sunday and start shouting. Tom's girlfriend, Penny, who had been in an adjacent room, rushed over to me.

"What happened here? Right here?" I pointed down at the floor where I stood. Penny looked at me curiously then took a deep breath.

"A female teacher lived here about fifty years ago. I was told by a previous owner that the woman was cooking here in the kitchen when her dress caught on fire. She burned to death...right where you're standing," Penny said.

I was speechless. I had had a physical reaction exactly where a woman had burned to death. How was this possible? Again, I was asking myself a question that I couldn't answer. And once again, a psychic experience left me with a case of anxiety on Easter Sunday.

A second visit to the house was scheduled for Mom's 80th birthday party. The party had been postponed from February until April due to a snowstorm the day before her birthday. Needless to say, the prospect of a second visit to the two-hundred-year-old house where the owner had burned to death filled me with anxiety.

I drove that day to my brother's house using secondary country roads. I wanted to take in the springtime beauty along the Connecticut River. Nevertheless, I just couldn't forget the story of the woman who had died in the kitchen. I kept telling myself that the visit this year would be different. I was going to the house to celebrate my mother's 80th birthday. I had no intention of reigniting an unpleasant conversation about a horrible accident. My family was not interested in upsetting conversations, especially at a special event like an 80th birthday party.

I entered through the front door, moving as quickly as I could past the kitchen area where the woman had died fifty years earlier. I reached the dining room without incident. *Hooray!* I laughed to myself. The family was cramped together in the tiny living room. The wooden plank floor squeaked each time someone took a step. Sunshine poured into the room through the handmade glass windowpanes.

Suddenly, I felt a deep chill. The warmth of the dining room was somehow drawn away from me. Despite the brilliant sunlight, it was cooler than the outdoor temperature. In an instant, my skin became very cold. I released a deep breath and noticed a slight filmy apparition. It was very faint and only noticeable to me. I was frightened.

"What's the matter?" my sister Lenore asked.

"Why is it so cold in here?" I asked.

"Seems okay to me," she said, then moved closer to me.

"I feel it now. It's only cold where you're standing," she said, remaining close to me.

The temperature directly around me had definitely fallen. I felt some type of energy holding me stationary. I released another deep breath. The faint condensation remained. Within a minute, the temperature had returned to normal. It ended as quickly as it had begun. Lenore and I looked at each other with amazement.

"I'm not crazy...am I?" I asked.

"I think it was her...the lady who burned to death. I smelled smoke when I walked in here today." Lenore said. I nodded in agreement. I realized then that I was not alone with my abilities.

"Let's keep this to ourselves," I said.

Still a little shaken, Lenore and I went to the dining table and poured ourselves a glass of wine. We didn't discuss what had happened because we weren't able to explain it to ourselves.

Stories about hauntings make for interesting television, but when you find yourself in the middle of an actual event, it hits you physically, emotionally, and energetically. You can't explain it away. Unfortunately, my mother's 80th birthday party left me with more anxiety and more unanswered questions.

20

Spirit Guide Visitation

Spirit Guide: an entity that remains a disincarnate spirit
who acts to protect living human beings

The towering figure of a Native American stood before me. He had my absolute attention. I couldn't take my eyes off of him. The only problem...I was sleeping!

In 1996, I had an evidential experience that changed my life forever. I consider myself a sound sleeper, but like most people, I do dream. However, I seldom remember anything in the morning. If I do, it usually makes little or no sense.

One night I experienced what I refer to as a Spirit Visitation. The emotional and energetic quality of a visitation is totally different than a dream—there is no comparison between the two experiences—but if I were to make one, I would say it's somewhat similar to the vast difference between listening to your favorite song on the radio versus a live performance. Other than that, I struggle to relate the intensity of what happened that night during my visitation. It was so memorable and powerful that when I think about the experience today, many years later, it's as if it happened just last night. My own spirit joined with that of the spirit visitor—of that, I am sure. I was overtaken by something that I hesitate to call an emotion—it was a joining of souls.

A male Native American figure entered my sleep state. In fact, he pushed himself into a dream that I was already having. It felt like a dream within a dream. However, within minutes I realized it was *something much different.*

I felt the power of this entity take center stage. I saw clearly what was happening and became aware that I was involved in a clairvoyant experience. I was the captive audience. He was speaking to me and to me alone. It was clear he wanted my undivided attention. Although I was asleep, I felt more awake in his presence than I do during the day. As difficult as it is for me to understand, at the time, I fully comprehended what was happening. There was no confusion, nor did I have any fear. I was in a meeting from which I did not necessarily want to wake. I was extremely interested in what he had to say. "Otherworldly" would be the only word I could use to describe what was happening.

He spoke directly to me but not with words. It was definitely some type of telepathic communication. He was a large male with fine features, coffee-colored skin and long dark hair. I was able to hear his words as he communicated from his mind to mine. I listened carefully and intently.

The fellow told me he had never actually lived on Earth but had been with me since birth. His words spoke to my heart. (The thought that he was possibly a guardian angel crossed my mind the next day.)

Suddenly, the mode of communication changed—he showed me a vision. Up to that point, this fellow *was* the vision—something else was happening. It was very much like watching a movie. I was shown the grassy fields behind the house where I lived as a child—an Indian village. The tipis were not conventional like I had seen in Western movies. Rather, they were round huts. I was able to look closely enough to see that the huts were made of sticks and animal skins. The Indian spirit said the year was 1636 and that the Indians that lived there were sick and dying, though I didn't see anyone dying during the vision. When it was over, I asked him only one question.

"What is your name?"

I had had no difficulty understanding the words he had spoken to me as they were telepathically communicated in English. However, he answered my only question in a different language. It was an odd-sounding word in a guttural language I had never heard before. Before I could ask for clarification, he was gone.

Spirit Guide Visitation

I remained asleep for a few more hours and awoke the next morning with a full recollection of the visitation. *My God! What the heck happened last night?* I felt a rush of emotion. I was exhilarated, but at the same time, in a state of disbelief. Immediately, the names and dates mentioned by the Native American flooded my mind as if I had just heard them—like everything had been imprinted onto my memory. Even his strange foreign name echoed in my head. I grabbed a pencil and wrote down the letters U-N-K-T-A-H—as close as I could phonetically get to what his had name sounded like.

That night changed my view of this world and reality itself. Nothing was what it seemed to be. I'm not saying that I completely embraced the existence of another reality that day, but it did get me thinking. I accepted that there was something else going on, something just beyond the veil of what I could normally comprehend. As hard as had I tried, I could no longer deny that there had to be another spiritual reality accessible to human beings. Whatever or whomever had been trying to get my attention since I was eight years old, now had it!

During the following months, I searched textbooks and eventually the Internet and was easily able to validate that in 1636, Quinnipiac Indians had lived in my neighborhood. Nearly all of them died from an illness contracted from the early settlers of New Haven, Connecticut. While I felt relieved that the historical information delivered to me during my visitation was verifiable and correct, I still had a great deal of anxiety and confusion around trying to understand how exactly a visitation could occur. *If a spirit world really does exist, why do these strange things only happen to me? Will I ever find out who Unktah really is?*

21

Religious Visions

"The hearing ear, and the seeing eye—the Lord hath made even both of them."

—Proverbs 20:12

I returned from Cape Cod earlier than planned. It was Labor Day weekend 1997, and I had a meeting with the State University of New York Department of Nursing regarding their nurse practitioner curriculum. I had arranged that Friday to meet with the nursing administrator at an uptown Manhattan restaurant, near the Museum of Natural History.

I parked across the street from the museum and waited for the traffic to clear on Central Park West. As I waited for the light to change, I saw a woman across the street about thirty yards from where I stood. She was short and dressed in what looked like a white nun's habit. It was white with blue horizontal stripes across the front. We stared directly at one another from opposite sides of the street.

My first thought was, *This is an actress dressed up to look like Mother Teresa. Maybe the museum has a special religious art show going on?* I couldn't imagine why Mother Teresa would be on Manhattan's Upper West Side, standing alone on a sidewalk.

As the traffic began to subside, the woman's dress began to shine a brilliant white in the noonday sun. I was mesmerized. More than a minute passed while I stared, transfixed. I tried to make sense of what the heck I was looking at. It didn't seem real. I needed to watch out for moving traffic before I started across the street, but I couldn't look away from her.

I crossed the first lane of traffic, then stopped in the middle of the street to wait for a yellow school bus to pass—I was about halfway to where she was standing. *How is the sunlight making her glow?* I wondered. My mind raced. I couldn't figure out what was going on. I could not understand who or what I was looking at. The yellow bus passed between us. After it cleared my field of vision, she was gone. She had disappeared into thin air!

I got to the other side and looked everywhere. There were no cabs, cars, or people in the immediate area. The bus that had passed between us had not stopped, so there was no way she could have jumped onto it. The whole experience had happened in about ninety seconds, yet for way more than ninety seconds after that, I still felt stunned.

Confusion reigned. My heart raced. I couldn't wrap my mind around what had just happened. *What had I just witnessed?* I checked to see if there was a religious event at the museum. Nope. *Maybe Mother Theresa was in town, visiting the museum?* I searched for a logical explanation. There was nothing logical about what I had just witnessed.

Prior to that day, I had known very little about Mother Teresa. I had seen photos of her in the news when she met Princess Diana in the early nineties. Other than that, all I knew was that she was a nun who worked with the poor.

Throughout the next fifteen years, I shared the details of that apparition with only three people: my wife, and two mediums whom I knew very well. I had trouble believing what I had seen, so how could I expect others to believe it? Even today, despite having seen many apparitions throughout my life, this intense experience seems too unbelievable—I hesitated to even write about it. It was a major "why me?" moment but at the same time, something I later accepted as a very spiritual experience. Why would a religious person appear to me? Besides, all of the apparitions I'd seen were deceased people. As far as I knew, Mother Teresa was alive.

To this day, I have absolutely no idea why she appeared to me. In a strange way, I was in total acceptance of seeing and channeling loved ones who had passed but did not feel in the least bit worthy that Mother Teresa should appear to me. I wasn't a super religious person or even a good practicing Catholic. I was pretty ordinary when it came to religion. I have read stories about how people's lives were dramatically changed following a religious vision. For me, this was just another inexplicable event. I didn't change and become a fervent Catholic or begin to attend Sunday mass on a regular basis. I was only left with more unanswered questions and a little more anxiety.

I continued looking for reasons why she had showed herself to me. I grabbed at any potential reason or connection. Shortly after that Friday in September 1997, I learned that one of our Bronx health centers provided health care to nuns of the Missionaries of Charity—the Order founded by Mother Teresa. I was also told that Mother Teresa often took walks in Central Park across the street from The Museum of Natural History. This was comforting to hear, but not any great explanation why she had shown herself to me.

Eighteen years later, the most amazing piece of information was revealed to me. The lunch meeting I had that day was on the Friday after Labor Day, 1997. I had purposely returned early from Cape Cod for the lunch meeting with the nursing administrator. On the day of my meeting, I arrived early, as I always do for business meetings.

The apparition in front of The Museum of Natural History was sometime between 11:00 a.m. and 11:30 a.m. Mother Teresa had passed away (in India) on that same Friday, September 5th, 1997 sometime between 11:00 a.m. and 12:00 noon, Eastern Time. She passed nearly the exact moment I saw her that morning in Manhattan!

Now, years later, I have developed a sincere appreciation for nuns who devote their lives to taking care of the sick and pray daily for the souls here on Earth. I try to support these "angels on Earth" as I refer to them, whenever I am able. I feel that their prayers can be extremely healing. I was not always aware of this throughout my life nor did I ever give it much thought. Now I do. I have witnessed nuns' praying for a family member resulting in the shrinkage of a cancer tumor. Doctors were unable to give a medical explanation as to how or why this happened. I have to admit that something within me has changed. Did my experience that morning have something to do with my revised understanding of those who lead a spiritual life? Possibly...

22

A Second Dream Visitation

"Pure water will one day be extremely rare."

—Unktah, my spirit guide, 1998

Unktah, my spirit guide, returned in 1998. It had been two years since his first contact. The circumstances were much the same. He interrupted my sleep during the middle of the night. On this occasion, he spoke to me about the water on planet Earth. I have to admit that back in 1998, I had not given much thought to the water supply on the planet. It was definitely *not* a topic that was foremost in my mind. Nobody I knew was concerned with Earth's supply of water in the nineties. Today is a different story: recently, in 2022, the Canadian government reported that 40% of the world's population does not have sufficient clean water.

In 1998, Unktah told me that people on this planet were becoming ill from impurities in the water. He showed me ground water flowing over the eastern part of the United States.

"As the water moves, it picks up invisible impurities from the Earth's surface. Man-made impurities build up in the soil and eventually run into the water. These substances should not be in water. These substances should not be in human beings." As he spoke, I was able to see the water he was referring to. To my eyes, the water appeared clean. He was adamant that the water was not clean but impure. I heard his grave concern for humans who would become ill because of the water problem.

He continued, "Pure water will one day be extremely rare—in the not-too-distant future, water will be as precious as gold," he said.

Unktah then showed me another vision that had nothing to do with water. It continues to disturb me to this day. I was above Earth, looking down from a vantage point above the Mediterranean Sea. From the eastern end of the Mediterranean toward India, the land was engulfed in orange flames. I did not become frightened. I was merely a passive observer. During all the years that have passed since this vision in 1998, nothing has occurred in that part of the world that even comes close to what I was shown. I had to go to a map to refresh my memory while writing this that the orange flames I saw stretched across Lebanon, Israel, Turkey, Syria, Iraq, Iran, Afghanistan, Pakistan, and on to India. Needless to say, it encompassed a huge portion of the globe. The Mideast wars that have been fought since 1997 are dwarfed by what I was shown that night. The vision haunts me. I was never one to try to predict the future. Hopefully human beings will call upon the love in their hearts to overcome any negative events that could disrupt mankind in such a way. Unktah gave no explanation why he showed me the vision.

A week later, I arrived at our hospital office for my usual midweek meeting with the physicians who were members of a fellowship program I was leading at the time. I walked through the hospital lobby past the Latina woman who worked the front desk. Mariana had a way of making everyone feel at home before they began what was often a long twelve-hour workday. She often spoke to me in Spanish, knowing that I had worked in Spain for many years.

"Dr. Deary, do you know that you have an American Indian with you?" she asked.

"What? What do you mean?" I replied.

"He's always walking behind you. I see him with you every time you come here. He's a very large Indian spirit. He's one of your guardian angels," she said.

"Oh! Okay," I said. I was so surprised, I couldn't respond further.

I took the elevator upstairs. I was literally shaking. I gave my morning presentation, but my mind was elsewhere. A woman I had known for years had just scared the hell out of me. *Thank God there was no one else in the lobby to overhear what she said,* I thought. The

A Second Dream Visitation

rest of the day, I couldn't stop thinking about the two dream visitations I had had with Unktah. I had *never mentioned* those visitations to anyone...not one person...least of all the people I *worked* with. Now, out of the blue, the front desk woman saw and described the same Indian, walking behind me. *This is crazy stuff*, I thought.

As much as I wanted to question Mariana, I decided to not talk with her about what she'd said to me. The last thing I wanted was for it to get around the hospital.

Prior to the development of the Internet, I had searched in bookstores all around Manhattan—I was on an endless mission to find the identity of Unktah. After all, he had appeared to me twice in dream visitations, providing evidence of some things that I was able to validate, and someone could actually *see him with me*. Part of me wanted to confirm that this spirit guide actually did exist. Another part of me wished that none of this metaphysical stuff were true. It was too much to handle. What if it were real? That would prove that another world really did exist! I wasn't sure I wanted to find that out.

Years later, in 2012, I Googled the name Unktah as I had numerous times before. For the first time, the spell-check popped up on my screen. "Unktah" became "Untunktahe!" I couldn't believe my eyes. My sixteen-year search was over. The online article that popped up on my screen was entitled "Water Mythology." It explained that the Lakota Sioux believed Untunktahe to be a Water God and Great Spirit with magical powers.

Untunktahe had expressed a great concern for the preservation of water on the planet. *A Water Spirit appeared to me in a dream to tell me about water*, I thought. *This can't be a coincidence!* My mind shot back to my childhood and my near-death drowning in my uncle's swimming pool when I was two years old. My aunt had pulled me out. I was told that my body was completely blue. Maybe I really did drown...I don't know...did I die? My mind raced. I wondered if being saved from the water had anything to do with the Water Spirit? Was

Untunktahe my guardian angel? Did he save my life that day in the swimming pool? I grasped for answers. My head was spinning with more questions—questions I couldn't answer.

23

Uninvited Dinner Guests

"Nearly one-in-five U.S. adults (18%) say they've seen or been in the presence of a ghost. An even greater share – 29% – say they have felt in touch with someone who has already died."

—The Pew Research Center, 2009

My wife was born and raised in the Steeltown suburbs of Pittsburgh. Sallie and I met in Florida in 2000 and were married a few years later. We decided to visit Pittsburgh so I could learn a bit about her hometown. One night in February we arranged to meet her high school girlfriend and husband in the Shiloh Restaurant that stood high on a hill, overlooking the business district of downtown Pittsburgh. Nearly everything in the hill area of Mt. Washington had been gentrified except the two-hundred-year-old building that housed the Shiloh Restaurant.

The four of us sat down for dinner at a round antique table covered with a white tablecloth. Below us, the city of Pittsburgh and its three rivers was visible through the clear winter day. Light snow began to fall as we ordered a bottle of wine for the table. We couldn't believe it when the waiter told us he had just sold the *last bottle* of red wine. *This is a first*, I thought to myself. *How can a restaurant be out of wine?* Then, much to my surprise, he offered to walk to the corner wine shop to get us a bottle—it would be on the house. He put a basket of bread on the table and said he'd be back in ten minutes. I excused myself to the men's room to wash my hands.

As I headed past the staircase that led up to the second floor, I looked up and froze in my tracks. *It was happening again.* Six cloudy figures were walking up the staircase beside me. They appeared fuzzy, so I couldn't tell if they were male or female. Each walked very slowly, bent forward from the waist like they were elderly. Though I could only see them for five or six seconds, I couldn't believe my eyes. Again.

Here I was, on my first visit to Pittsburgh, trying to enjoy myself with friends, and spirits show up. Why did this keep happening? It was becoming a nuisance and I was getting angry. *People are not supposed to be seeing spirits when they're out enjoying themselves.* It was not fun for me—yet *another* anxiety moment.

I continued on to the men's room before returning to the table where Sallie sat alone. The others had left to explore the historic restaurant while they waited for the waiter to return with the wine. Sallie saw the look on my face, but before she could ask if I was okay, I explained what had happened. Before she could comment, the waiter returned with two bottles of red wine. He was covered in snow and apologetic that we had had to wait.

"Thank you for going out in this weather," I paused, accepting his nod. "Tell me, was this building always a restaurant?"

"Well, it's been a restaurant for a very long time," he replied.

Sallie looked at me. She knew that I was searching for some historical evidence to support what I had seen. Our friends returned then and joined in on the conversation. They too had an historic interest in the neighborhood, but for very different reasons than mine.

"Years ago, this building was a private home," the waiter continued.

None of what he said resonated with what I had seen. When I saw the spirits on the staircase, I had the distinct feeling that they did not live in or own the house.

"A customer once told me that a doctor lived here a long time ago. I think he saw patients upstairs on the second floor," the waiter continued.

That's it, I thought. I felt that this information represented what I had seen. The slow-moving figures, bent forward, were not elderly people. They were patients who were ill. Although I couldn't prove any of this, I believed that these individuals had passed away up on the second floor. And, like so many times before, I was left asking myself, *Why me?*

24

The Beach House Haunting

Apparition: an unusual or unexpected sight: a phenomenon; also, a ghostly figure

My life was about to change forever. In the summer of 2007, Sallie and I rented a beach house on Saugatuck Island along the Connecticut coastline. Our plan was to rent while we decided whether or not we wanted to relocate permanently to Manhattan or remain in the Connecticut suburbs.

We were scheduled to meet with Lester, the caretaker of the beach house, at 9:00 a.m. on Wednesday to tour the property. The availability of beachfront property during August was unheard of. Everyone wanted to be on Long Island Sound during the summer months. Finding a vacancy was like winning the lottery, so I knew the house would be rented in a matter of hours. For the life of me, I couldn't understand why a family would leave their beach house in the middle of summer. I considered it a stroke of good luck.

Lester met us at the house right on time. It was completely furnished so all we would have to do was bring our television. He showed us the kitchen and instructed us on the use of shut-off valves, electric boxes, the oil furnace, and gave us other assorted household tips. Though he didn't say, it, I got the message that giving us the information was to ensure that we wouldn't call him with problems in the middle of the night.

"Looks like the last tenant left a few things behind. What's with all the kid's toys on the kitchen floor?" Sallie asked.

"Yeah, sorry about that. The owner of the house lived here with her two children. She left quickly and moved to another house she owns off-island," Lester said.

I went into the dining room while Sallie and Lester headed to the laundry room. The dining room, located in the interior of the house, was windowless and therefore dimly lit, even during the morning hours. I stood at the entrance to the dining room and ran my hand up and down the wall, searching for a light switch.

I fumbled in the dark and was startled when a man walked in front of me, right past the dining room table—I thought at first that it was Lester. My fingers finally found the light switch. Within seconds, Sallie and Lester were entering the dining room from the opposite side.

"Sorry again about those toys," Lester was saying. "It was just such a quick turnaround. Anything else I can help you with today?"

In my confusion, I was speechless. It clearly could not have been Lester that I just saw. No one had been in the dining room except me. My heart pounded in my chest.

"No. No, I'm good," I finally answered.

"I told Lester we're ready to sign the lease," Sallie said.

"Yes. Okay. It's a great location," I replied, still staring beyond the dining room table.

Sallie could tell something had happened. Throughout our years together, I had always shared my paranormal experiences with her. She understood and was never frightened. Once again, those familiar phrases bounced around inside my racing mind, *Not again! Why me?*

"I'll leave my number on the kitchen table. Call me if you need anything. Don't call the owner," Lester instructed. Shortly after Lester left, Sallie and I drove off-island to get lunch.

"You won't believe what I saw in the house," I said, my voice shaking.

"I can only guess?" Sallie said.

This was the first time an apparition had occurred within our personal space...in the house we were planning to live in. This episode didn't frighten me—this time I was *angry*. I *did not* want a spirit in my house.

I considered not telling Sallie the details. Why tell a story that would inevitably change the mood of the day? It should be a happy day.

We had just rented a beautiful summer beach house. Instead, I was in the middle of another day of confusion and anxiety. I felt selfish that I even wanted to discuss the encounter with Sallie. It was not *fun* or *interesting*. Seeing a full body apparition is about as shocking and confusing as it can get!

"Sallie, I saw a guy in the dining room. He walked right in front of me toward the office at the far end of the room. I saw him as clearly as I see you right now," I said. "He was a little shorter than I am, with thick black hair combed in a kind of Elvis Presley style. He wore a black sweater and black trousers and his skin was very light. Sal, he walked right through the wall!" I said.

"You saw all of that? Black clothes in a dark room?" Sallie asked.

I had no explanation. How did I "see" so much in a room that was so dimly lit? I couldn't explain it to myself, let alone to Sallie.

"I don't know. Sal, do you think we should still move into this place?" I asked. "Isn't there supposed to be a strict separation between the living and dead?" In the end, we agreed not to let it ruin our summer. We agreed to stick with our decision and rent the beach house.

By mid October, it had begun to get cold. We turned the heat on for the first time just before Halloween. Due to multiple additions, there was both oil heat and electric heat in various areas of the house. Despite the dual heating systems, we were never able to get the living room warm. After a few repair visits that proved fruitless, we reluctantly stopped using the living room during the cooler months.

One November afternoon, Sallie started to organize some of the papers in my office adjacent to the dining room. She opened one of the desk drawers and found some tax forms and photos belonging to the homeowner.

"She must have been in a big hurry to leave behind their tax information. Remember all the toys on the kitchen floor? Jim, look at this photo! It's a picture of the guy you described during your apparition—exactly like you said!"

I took the photo from Sallie. It showed a middle-aged man with thick hair combed back like Elvis. He was wearing a black sweater and trousers. His hair was slightly grey. He looked a few years older than he was when he had appeared to me, but it was definitely the same man I saw in the dining room.

I felt somewhat relieved. Every time I'd seen an apparition, I wondered if it were real. There was always doubt—that my mind had created the vision. I had lingering thoughts that something was wrong with my eyes or, God forbid, my brain! It was validating, knowing that hard evidence existed to support that I had seen an apparition. I began to feel a little less crazy.

A few days later, I was in the backyard, giving the lawn a final mowing before winter, when Lester stopped by to ask how things were going at the house. I was happy to see him. He was nice guy who had lived on the island most of his life. The neighbors trusted him to watch their homes during the off-season, so I was comfortable enough with him to share what had happened in the house.

"You remember the first day you showed us around? I saw something in the dining room," I said. Lester looked up at me with dark Italian eyes. He wasn't at all surprised. He seemed to know where I was going with the conversation, but he remained silent.

"What's going on here?" I asked. He took a deep breath.

"The husband died in the house about twelve months ago," he said. "His wife told me that she felt her husband's presence behind her all the time. It got to be too much for her, so she took the kids and moved to another house she owns across town," Lester said.

"Where exactly did he die?" I asked.

"Your bedroom. But don't worry. She had me and my son replace the mattress."

What Lester said didn't come as a surprise. It had certainly crossed my mind that I had seen an apparition of someone who died in the house.

"My son will never go near this beach house again," Lester continued.

"What? Why?" I asked.

"He got scared out of his wits. We were rearranging the furniture in the living room and dining room the night before you arrived, on July 31st, so the place would look presentable. My son couldn't explain what happened to him, only that he's never coming back here again," Lester explained.

Now it made sense to me why the house had become available on August 1st. Something scared both Lester's son and the woman who was living in the house. She was so scared that she left with her children right in the middle of summer. My heart went out to her for her loss and for what she'd had to endure, both his loss and then what followed after her husband's passing. It didn't seem right. She lost her husband, then was frightened out of her wits by his spirit. This wasn't supposed to happen.

Don't boundaries exist between the two worlds? She had to leave her waterfront home in the middle of summer—death's final insult. Don't those who passed over want their loved ones to continue living happy lives...lives free from the fear of ghosts? These were more questions for which I had no answer.

Ghost stories may make for amusing theatre but when someone experiences the real thing, it's far from amusing. It scares the hell out of you, but not necessarily right away. At first it seems like an incredibly interesting event. But afterward, when the realization hits you that you've experienced an objective apparition of a poltergeist...a spirit that lives inside your house, you can become overwhelmed. It changes your perspective of reality. Everything you once held sacred...everything you believed about life and death, all comes into question.

Privately, most people don't believe this phenomenon really exists. It's too much of a challenge to their beliefs, religion, customs, and personal experience. They pass it off as imagination, projection, magical thinking, or any number of other sophisticated psychological terms. Some people are threatened by ideas and beliefs that oppose their own. The existence of a spirit in a home can affect people in many different ways. On this occasion, I shared in their anxiety.

Poltergeist: a noisy usually mischievous ghost responsible for unexplained noises (such as rappings).

One December evening, Sallie and I went to bed a little earlier than usual. It was close to 9:30 p.m. on a Tuesday. We were warmer watching TV in bed as, despite the expensive heating bills, other areas of the house were quite cold.

As soon as I turned off the TV, we heard the sound of footsteps on the staircase—they were quite loud. I sat up, overtaken with panic as I turned on the bedside lamp. Sallie looked fearful—we assumed someone had broken into the house. Instinctively, I ran out of the bedroom to the bottom of the staircase. The footsteps stopped. It was absolutely silent. I figured the intruder had reached the upstairs bedroom.

My whole body was charged with adrenaline. Not thinking of how much danger I could be in, I ran into the kitchen and grabbed a steak knife, then slowly started up the staircase. Reaching the top, I could clearly see that both bedrooms were empty.

"Are you all right? Should I call the police?" Sallie yelled.

"No. No, there's no one here," I shouted. "Those footsteps were going *up* the staircase? Right? Is that what you heard?"

"Definitely. Someone went *up*stairs," Sallie said. I knew that we couldn't *both* be crazy. We had heard someone walking up the staircase. There was no doubt about it. Every step was slow, deliberate, and clear. We were scared.

The next day I was physically and emotionally exhausted. That evening, we continued to discuss what had happened the night before. We searched for a logical explanation. Maybe it was an animal. Nothing made any sense.

The following night, we went to bed around 10:30 p.m. after the local news. No sooner had the room become dark, we heard the same footsteps on the staircase. We sat up in bed and counted thirteen steps moving from the bottom to the top of the staircase. I couldn't believe this was happening again. I went to the bottom of the stairs and slowly made my way upstairs. Again, no one was there. Like the night before, I continued to check all the doors, locks, windows, and closets. Everything was secure. Neither of us could explain what we heard. We couldn't yet wrap our heads around the idea that the man who had died in our bedroom was walking up the staircase to his children's bedrooms.

During the next few weeks, we heard our night visitor on no fewer than six occasions. It became an almost freakish game. We'd lie in bed and count out the thirteen footsteps banging up the wood staircase. There were always thirteen, no more, and no less. On nights we didn't hear footsteps, there were other noises that sounded like animals running across the ceiling. I had the roof, gutters, and attic checked for animals—nothing there! Nothing made sense.

During the next few weeks, our worry escalated into anxiety. I thought it was all my fault. Maybe *I* was the problem. Maybe I was haunted? After all, I was the one who had the history of seeing apparitions. Could I somehow be attracting spirits? My thinking only added to my stress. It became increasingly difficult to push everything out of my mind and focus on my work. Some kind of force or intelligence had been trying to get my attention. They certainly had it now!

We spent Christmas and New Year's at our condo in Florida. The Florida weather helped alleviate the stress of our beach house nightmare. We tried not to discuss what had happened. We had a mutual unspoken explanation. Not a logical explanation, but nevertheless, an explanation. We had a ghost living in our house: a) the owner had died in our in our bedroom, b) I saw his apparition, c) the photo in the desk confirmed that it was him, d) his wife had felt his presence so strongly that she and the kids had to move out, and e) something had really scared the caretaker's son. Everything pointed to the fact that we definitely had *a ghost living in our house.* What the evidence did not answer was, *why me?*

25

The Ghost Speaks

"James, the spirit spoke to you because you're a medium."

—Mavis Pittilla, Pompton Lakes, NJ, 2009

A few months passed without having to deal with any poltergeist activity in the beach house. Sallie and I were looking forward to spending spring and summer on the island. Months earlier, I had won the local golf championship and had become friends with many of the local residents. After a lifetime of living and working around the world, I finally felt like a member of a community.

One night, around 10:00 p.m., I was jolted awake again by the sound of footsteps on the staircase. This time, something felt very different. The bedroom became unbelievably cold. It was even colder than it had been that day during my mom's 80th birthday party, when Lenore and I were confronted by the female spirit who had burned to death in the kitchen. An "electric" atmosphere had filled our bedroom. Once again, Sallie and I counted out the chilling sound of thirteen footsteps as someone walked up the second-floor staircase. I can only describe the feeling that enveloped me as "electric cold." The footsteps ceased and silence filled our bedroom.

"What are you doing here?" I *heard* a voice ask. "What are you doing in my house? Where is my family?" The male voice blared at me from the hallway that connected our bedroom to the kitchen. Instinctively, I replied to the voice with my inner mind.

"Your wife doesn't live here anymore. Do you remember that you died?"

Again—total silence. The room temperature then quickly warmed and the electric energy I had experienced was no longer present. In that specific moment, my life changed forever. I was well aware that I had just successfully *communicated* with a spirit from the other side of death.

I got out of bed, turned on the lights, and headed down the hallway to the kitchen. I was momentarily gripped again by that same electric energy. This time, it felt like I had been hit with a bolt of lightning. When I got back into bed with Sallie, I felt dazed and confused.

"Sallie, did you hear all that?" I asked.

"Hear what?' she said.

"A spirit just spoke to me. I actually heard the words outside of myself. This was not a mental impression inside my head. Sal, I *heard* his words. He *spoke* to me—in his own words! Are you sure you didn't hear anything?" Sallie shook her head.

My first impulse was to call the owner of the house to tell her that her husband was here and that he had communicated with me. Sallie quickly convinced me to forget that idea.

I was overwhelmed with nervous excitement. I had *heard a voice speak!* This was crazy. It's not supposed to happen. *Had* it actually happened? Maybe I had an overactive imagination or something was wrong with me? Again, I searched for an explanation. Thoughts and fears raced through my mind. I didn't want to accept what had happened. But there was little doubt that *it did* happen. Very few words were spoken during my communication with the spirit, yet somehow, I immediately *knew* a great deal about this man who had passed away: I *felt* that he was very intelligent, good looking, with an energetic and nervous type of personality. He was ambitious, able to fill a room with his presence, and in good physical shape. More importantly, he loved his wife and kids beyond imagination. He also loved his life on this island—raising his kids here had made him happy. And, I definitely knew that he had passed in the house.

Weeks later, the neighbors began to come out of their winter seclusion to start cleaning up their yards. I wanted to learn more about the man who had spoken to me from the other side of death. So, one Saturday afternoon, I followed their lead and raked up some of the leaves and twigs left behind by the winter winds. As I was picking up some small branches, someone called over to me.

"Hey, Champ! Didn't know you were living on the island. When did you move in?" He looked familiar—I had seen him before, at the golf club.

"I've been here since August," I called back. I headed across the street to say hello. He shook my hand and congratulated me on winning the club championship.

"Did you know the fellow who owned my house?" I asked after some small talk.

"Yeah, he was a good friend," he said.

"Was his name Westie?" I asked. I didn't know how I knew the spirit's name.

"Yes. Actually, his name was Wesley, but his friends called him Westie. I guess you knew him too?" he said.

"No. No, I never met him," I said hesitantly.

I considered ending the conversation, but I had to find out more about the man who died in the house. I needed to validate everything that the spirit had allowed me to know and hear.

"Was Wesley a high energy type of guy—like the nervous type?" I asked.

"That's him. I really miss him. You sure you didn't know him?" he asked.

I shook my head no and quickly changed the subject to golf. However, the neighbor continued on later to say that Westie's wife felt so much grief and sadness that she and the kids had left the island. It was clear that he knew nothing about her being followed by her husband's ghost as Lester had told me.

A few days later, Sallie and I were in the kitchen having dinner when we heard the sound of a cat meowing. We stopped eating and got up to see if a stray cat had found its way into the house, but we didn't find anything out of the ordinary. The meowing continued.

"That's coming from your office," Sallie said.

My mother had given Sallie a toy cat for Christmas. It was a battery-operated toy with a motion sensor that enabled it to meow and shake its head and tail when switched on. The cat moved and meowed only when it detected the motion of someone passing directly in front of it. We kept it on the desk in my office next to the dining room.

I walked through the dining room and into my office. As I approached the toy cat, the meowing stopped. I picked it up and checked the power switch. The switch was in the OFF position! I turned the switch back on to test if it was in working order. Then I walked in front of the cat's motion sensor. The cat meowed and moved its tail. Then, to test it further, I turned it off again and walked in front of its sensor. Nothing happened, no movement...the toy was in perfect working order.

Okay, I said to myself, *what exactly is going on here?* Believe me, not for one minute did I want to entertain the idea that the ghost was causing this. *Please, please, I need a rational explanation.*

I went back to the kitchen and saw the look of desperation on Sallie's face. We both knew what was happening. During the next two weeks, we heard meows on two more occasions. It was always during the night. Then, about a week later—as if things couldn't get worse—the footsteps on the staircase began again. Every time this happened, it hit me like an emotional hammer to my head. It depleted every ounce of my energy. I had had enough!

On April 1st, we broke our lease and left the beach house. Our real estate agent relocated us across town. We eventually heard through friends that the beach house quickly leased to another family but that they had left within weeks. I could only guess why.

I experienced too many sleepless nights and days of anxiety at that house. Real fatigue had set in, and I was angry. What should have been a wonderful year was a real-life nightmare. However, in a strange way, I felt a debt of gratitude to the beach house spirit. My communication with Westie led me on the path to take a first step to accepting that I was indeed a psychic medium.

From the age of eight, I had had experiences that I was never able to explain. The beach house spirit provided me with evidence that another world did exist and that I was able to communicate with it. It seemed my time for avoidance might have passed.

26

Even in Death, We Do Not Part

"I shall be more useful to you in heaven than on Earth."

—St. Teresa of Lisieux, 1897

The Broadway theatre didn't open its doors until 7:00 p.m. Sallie and I had a few hours of free time before the show began, so we walked up Fifth Avenue to St. Patrick's Cathedral. I had visited the cathedral on a number of occasions and welcomed its peaceful refuge in the hectic city. I'd seen many of the great cathedrals of the world during my years working in Europe as a musician, but my favorite cathedral was right here in Manhattan, just a few blocks from my office.

We made our way to the rear of the church, stopping at the white marble alter devoted to the memory of St. Teresa of Lisieux, a French nun. We were kneeling for a short prayer when I noticed a tall priest heading down the marble walkway directly behind me. I waited for him to pass before taking a step back from the altar. I continued to watch while he walked toward the front of the cathedral. Other than his height he looked much like the other priests, dressed in a plain black tunic.

"Sallie, that priest was really tall, wasn't he?" I asked.

"What priest?" Sallie asked.

"The guy that just walked behind us while we knelt at the altar," I said.

"Nobody walked behind us," Sallie insisted.

"Sallie! A tall priest just walked right behind us as we knelt at St. Teresa's altar. How could you have missed him?" Sallie just stared at me. She understood what had happened before I did.

"It must have been another apparition," she said.

"No, no. I saw him clearly. He was really tall," I said.

I didn't want to accept what Sallie was suggesting. Inevitably, I always ask myself if I'm crazy. Normally when I saw a spirit, I would *know* it was someone who had passed. This was different. The priest looked like any other live human being. Quickly, I walked to the front of the cathedral to look for him. I checked the pews and doorways. He seemed to have vanished into thin air. I reminded myself that I wasn't crazy and that I had been through this before. Nevertheless, this time I had trouble accepting it.

"You can do some research. Maybe a really tall priest used to work here at St. Patrick's Cathedral," Sallie said. She encouraged me to search for evidence. She knew my anxiety was greatly reduced when I found an answer, even if the answer didn't seem logical. Most of the time, the apparitions I saw were in some way connected to the location where I saw them.

A few weeks later, Sallie and I stopped again at the Cathedral. It was holiday season and we were headed to another Broadway show. A weekday mass was already in progress when we entered. It was unusual that nearly all of the twenty-four hundred seats were occupied. However, Archbishop Dolan, who had been recently elevated to cardinal, was officiating at the service. There were rumors that he was in the running to become the next pope, so many from the congregation attended the service to wish him well. We walked up the aisle on the right, looking for an empty pew. As we reached the front of the cathedral close to the altar, I turned for one last look behind me for a pew.

Fifteen rows back from the altar, on the inside of a pew, adjacent to a support column, I saw him. The tall priest was seated facing the altar, just like everyone else. Despite the fact that he was sitting down, he stood out in the crowd, a head taller than most. He wore the same black tunic. This time I had the distinct feeling that he was aware that I could see him. I turned and whispered to Sallie that the tall priest was there again, but when I turned back, his seat in the pew was empty.

My research failed to unearth anything about a tall priest who worked in the cathedral. Years had passed since the apparitions at St. Patrick's Cathedral, and in 2016, Karen, a member of my Mediumship Circle sent me an article about Mother Teresa of Calcutta. I had shared with Karen that I had had a vision of Mother Teresa of Calcutta years earlier in New York City in front of the Museum of Natural History. Karen told me that Mother Teresa had taken the name Teresa in honor of Saint Teresa of Lisieux, the French nun. I explained to Karen that I saw the tall priest at the Saint Teresa of Lisieux marble altar in St. Patrick's Cathedral.

Following my discussion with Karen, I decided to learn more about the life of Saint Teresa of Lisieux. I quickly learned that her religious mission in France was to pray for the success of priests who were sent away from France to do missionary work. I also learned about a priest named Father Roulland. Shortly after his ordination in France in 1896, Father Roulland was assigned to serve as a missionary priest in China. Before he left for China, he contacted the local convent and requested a nun be assigned to pray for his success. Saint Teresa of Lisieux was the nun assigned.

Saint Teresa corresponded with written prayers from her convent in France to Father Roulland in China for fourteen months. The correspondence ended abruptly due to the untimely death of Saint Teresa. She was only twenty-four years of age when she passed away.

I will never forget the day I entered the name Father Roulland into my Google search. The black and white image I saw on my computer screen brought tears to my eyes. There, in front of me, was the image of a very tall priest, dressed in a long black tunic. His long face and pronounced jaw were identical to the man I had seen pass behind me that day at St. Patrick's Cathedral as he walked by the alter of Saint Teresa. I had found the tall priest. I was humbled that I was given a beautiful gift from the other side.

Next to the photo of Father Roulland was the final note written to him by Saint Teresa shortly before her untimely death:

"I shall be more useful to you in heaven than on Earth. I am your Little Sister for eternity."

I reflected for a moment. I believe that Father Roulland, the tall priest, continues to look after his Little Sister Teresa at her altar in St. Patrick's Cathedral. I saw him there...twice! This was the first time an apparition had brought me such great *joy*. I was given proof that even in death, we do not part.

27

Spirit in the Boardroom

"An apparition at home, in church, and now at work!"

—J. Deary, Manhattan, 2009

The beach house experience had turned my life upside down. The ordeal had also impacted Sallie, the wife and children of the deceased, the caretaker, the caretaker's son, and the next family to rent the house after we left. But no one was affected as dramatically as I had been. The religious apparitions I experienced at St. Patrick's Cathedral had added more fuel to my metaphysical fire. I still had trouble accepting everything that had happened to me. My rational mind told me that it was all crazy. People don't *see* ghosts and especially the ghosts of religious people, do they? How was it possible? It must be some type of psychological projection in my mind. Despite these conversations I was having with myself, I *knew it all was true*. The events were not the result of magical thinking. There was always evidence regarding what I had seen and experienced.

Each experience helped bring into focus seemingly unrelated events that had been occurring since my childhood—events that were now becoming more frequent. The words of the Harvard astrologer thirty years earlier continued to echo in my mind. *Much later in your life, something will happen, and you will once again use your psychic gifts.*

One morning in early 2009, I arrived at work in Manhattan, ready for our monthly administrative management meeting. The organization I had co-founded had grown to nearly a thousand employees throughout our thirty health centers in the New York City area and up into the Northern Hudson River region. I had plenty on my mind with my day-to-day responsibilities and the challenges of helping to keep the organization viable. I certainly didn't want to be distracted by the metaphysical world.

Our Wednesday morning meeting was scheduled to last three hours. Typically, the agenda was divided among reports from our various health centers, followed by a strategic planning discussion. Twenty executives sat shoulder to shoulder around the board table.

This particular meeting seemed to drag on and on. I sat back in my chair and folded my arms across my chest, hoping the meeting would end soon. My mind wandered, and I was no longer able to focus on what was being said—I was zoned out and waiting for lunch break.

Suddenly, my attention was drawn to one of the administrators seated on the other side of the conference table. I *saw* the full-body apparition of a woman standing behind their right shoulder. I was spellbound. I sat up in my chair to make sure I wasn't sleeping. I was completely focused on the apparition. Unlike the fleeting image of the spirit I saw at the Connecticut beach house, this female apparition stood right behind the administrator for thirty or forty seconds.

She was tall and dressed in a beautiful light-purple skirt and matching jacket. It appeared to be a woven type of material and looked expensive. She wore a wide-brimmed hat like women sometimes wear to church. I knew the woman was strong, elegant, proud, and religious. Then, she spoke.

"Maxus!" the spirit called out, as if she were calling to someone she knew. I looked around to make sure that I was the only person at the table who had *heard* her. This spirit wanted me to let our administrator know she was there. The spirit mentioned additional information that led me to believe she was a close relative. For once, I was not shocked at seeing this apparition. Instead, there was a peaceful calm to the whole encounter.

Despite being left with a strong urge to tell the person what had happened, I didn't say a word for fear I would lose all professional credibility. After all, I was a co-founder of the organization.

I went home that night and told Sallie what had happened. She was adamant that I not discuss this with anyone. She said the administrator might think I had looked into their background. This was the first time that something paranormal had happened at work—things were getting out of control. I didn't know where to turn for help. What was certain was that I needed someone to put everything into perspective. I needed someone to tell me *that I wasn't crazy.*

About a month later, I arrived early for another meeting. It was scheduled away from Manhattan in one of our upstate health centers, near the Hudson River. I greeted the two people who had, like me, arrived early for the meeting. One of them was the administrator. I had not seen this individual since the meeting a month earlier. Needless to say, I was extremely curious about what the woman in spirit had said to me. The three of us engaged in small talk, waiting for the others to arrive for the meeting, and I gently moved the discussion to ancestry and family.

"Does the name Maxus mean anything to you?" I asked. They stared at me in utter surprise.

"Yes, that's my father's name. At least, Maxus is the nickname that everyone called him."

The administrator looked at me curiously. I was uncomfortable. Obviously, Maxus was a very unusual name. Though the look on their face clearly showed me that they couldn't figure out how I knew their father's nickname, they didn't ask, and I didn't say another word.

I immediately changed the conversation to company issues. Within a few minutes, others arrived, and the meeting began. I never followed up with the administrator about any of the information I heard from the spirit. I didn't want to appear foolish, nor did I want to upset them. On two subsequent Wednesday meetings, I saw the same apparition standing behind the individual. Both times, the spirit woman called out for Maxus.

That apparition was the straw that broke the camel's back. I was back to being angry. This was my workplace, my company, and my livelihood. This was an *invasion of my territory.* I had no idea why this was continually happening to me. I felt I could never reveal this part of myself to my colleagues in the medical field. I feared the loss of their respect and the loss of my credibility. This ability would have to remain in the closet. I didn't spend years earning a doctorate degree and co-founding a successful organization only to throw it all away on ghosts!

    I needed help.

28

DR. EDGEWORTH: ANOTHER SPIRIT GUIDE

"This fellow just showed up while I was sleeping."

—J. Deary

I am not an artist by any means, though I sometimes sketch pictures during my readings. No one told me to do it that way. It's just how I do it when I connect to the deceased spirit prior to making the call to my client. I take notes and draw pictures of everything that arrives into my clairvoyant vision. The drawings are basic simple stick-figures. I draw figures of both the deceased spirit and my client. As I draw, my pencil sometimes stops on specific areas of the figure, thus I psychically know that there is a medical problem in that area of their body. From my training, I try to only share medical information about the deceased person. However, if the medical issue is benign or has occurred in the past, I might mention it to my client—I'm more comfortable talking about medical events that have already happened. I generally refrain from describing events that are yet to occur. I am not a medical medium.

  A medium friend once told me that we sometimes have spirit guides who help us with various aspects of our readings. Her comment stuck with me. I wondered whether I could possibly have a guide that helped me "to see" medical issues since often my medical drawings were correct. I decided to spend time in prayer and meditation to ask my guide, Untunktahe, if I had other spirits working with me. I did this every night as I fell asleep. It had been many years since Untunktahe had visited me, but I figured maybe I could learn about other spirit helpers in the same way.

A few days later, I had a vivid psychic experience. A middle-aged dark-haired male entered my sleep state. It was not unlike what had happened when Untunktahe appeared. This fellow just showed up.

Despite being asleep, I was able to have a conversation with this spirit.

"Who are you?" I asked.

"I am Dr. Hedgeworth," he responded with an elegant British accent.

"You're a doctor from England?" I asked.

"I was...in 1898," he replied. That was the end of our conversation.

I awoke the next morning startled and amazed. I clearly recalled details of the visitation. Everything was fixed in my mind as if I had memorized the conversation, word by word.

Soon, doubt began to creep in. I asked myself if I had wished it to happen. Or had I set myself up for auto-suggestion prior to falling asleep? There was only one way to find out. I needed some proof. I had to find out if Dr. Hedgeworth had actually existed in England in 1898.

I figured I'd discover something as long as this wasn't a fabrication of my imagination. I entered "Dr. Hedgeworth, England, 1898," into my search engine. Nothing!

I told Sallie what had happened. She was always more optimistic than I was. She knew I had been receiving substantiated evidence during my readings. She also reminded me that it had taken quite a few years for me to identify that Untunktahe was my spirit guide. I tried multiple search engines before giving up.

As the weeks passed, I couldn't get the English accent out of my head. Somehow, I knew that this visitation had been the real thing. My readings evolved and I continued to develop more trust in my drawings. However, I still had not been able to verify that a Dr. Hedgeworth practiced medicine in England in 1898.

One afternoon, it dawned on me that maybe I hadn't heard the name Hedgeworth correctly—like what had happened when I tried to identify Untunktahe years ago. I grabbed my iPhone and began to search. I tried "Hedgewirth." Again, there was nothing. Then I tried omitting the H—and there it was—Dr. Edgeworth. Bingo!

F.H. Edgeworth, MD was a surgeon and professor of medicine in Great Britain. He spent most of his career at the British Royal Infirmary in Bristol about a hundred miles north of London. In 1898, he published an important study that is archived in Washington D.C. at the National Institutes of Health. I was ecstatic. I had found evidence of someone who spoke to me from the other side. I could not begin to describe the feeling I had, knowing I had two spirit guides. I was humbled. I began to more readily accept that I walked between two worlds. I wasn't alone. I had come to realize that no one is ever alone.

Sometimes, my abilities were too much to wrap my mind around. Why would a famous English surgeon want to be connected to a medium living in Florida? I was a beginner in the world of spirit—why wouldn't Dr. Edgeworth want to assist a real surgeon? And why help an unexperienced medium? Something pushed me to dig a little deeper into the life of Dr. Edgeworth.

Days later, I searched the web again. My screen opened to a display showing the January 1897 London edition of the *Journal of Psychical Research*. Francis H. Edgeworth, MD was listed as a researcher and author of a study on psychics who used divining rods to locate water beneath the ground.

I felt numb. My new spirit guide had an interest in neurology and the occult. He conducted research on psychics! I was overwhelmed with excitement and flabbergasted. It suddenly occurred to me that the Society for Psychical Research in Kensington London was the *very same building* I had wandered into back in 1970, the day I drove into London with teachers from the American School. And that was also the same day I learned about the famous medium, Gordon Higginson. Even today, I can't believe it. What are the odds of that happening? I was learning quickly that there are no coincidences in life.

29

Who Can Help Me?

"All mediums are psychics, but not all psychics are mediums."

—Mavis Pittilla, Pompton Lakes, NJ, 2009

If you look hard enough, you'll find whatever you need in New York City. That statement had always rung true for me, except—I couldn't find a teacher of mediumship. To be honest, I didn't look very hard. At that point in my life, I wasn't completely sure what a medium was. I had read somewhere that mediums are always psychic but that psychics aren't necessarily mediums—what the heck did that mean? At the time, that confused me. Later, I came to understand that a psychic communicates with the energy of a living person, and a medium is a psychic who also has an ability to communicate with the energy of a deceased spirit. This was my understanding as I made my entry into the world beyond the veil.

Manhattan has always had its share of psychics able to read the energy of living human beings. But finding a psychic medium, an individual able to communicate with the spirit of one who has passed, was another issue. And, to complicate things even further, most mediums weren't interested in helping someone like me who was struggling to make sense of the paranormal world. I needed to find a mediumship *teacher*.

I had heard through the grapevine that a teacher of a famous medium lived in Florida not far from our vacation condo. I thought that this might be a good place to start. While I deliberated about registering to train in Florida, I came across an article about a female medium in Boston. She was holding an introductory seminar in Andover,

Massachusetts for individuals who *thought* they might be having *spiritual experiences*. The article included a photo of the woman. I knew by looking at her face that I needed to be there with her. From early childhood, I'd received a combination of *feeling* and *knowing* information about a person just by seeing their face. I suppose this was an early expression of being a psychic.

For the next few hours, my logical mind kept telling me that Massachusetts was too far away. It would be more realistic to find a teacher in Manhattan near my office, or in Florida near my vacation condo. However, my knowing ability told me to visit the woman in Massachusetts. So, I went with my gut.

The following weekend, Sallie and I drove the two hundred miles to Andover. It was a beautiful spring weekend in 2008, and the town looked like a picture postcard of New England. Sallie would have plenty of time to explore the historic downtown village while I was in class for two hours.

As usual, I arrived early at the bookstore where the seminar was scheduled. The woman behind the counter motioned me toward the back room. A blonde-haired woman about my age sat alone, on one of the chairs that had been arranged in a circle. She was the same woman I had seen in the photo. She looked at me with kind blue eyes and asked, "So how long has Spirit been knocking on your door?" I laughed. *If she only knew,* I thought.

"They've been knocking all right. Actually, pounding!" I said. I told her about my experience at the Connecticut beach house when I had my first *communication* with a spirit apparition. I liked her immediately—she absolutely understood what I had been going through.

Lynnie introduced herself as a psychic medium and channel. She had trained for many years in Great Britain with some of the most respected mediumship tutors in the world. She mentioned that she had been a psychic medium for nearly thirty years and had published many books.

"This gift is your gift. I can only help guide you and share with you what my tutors have shared with me. Someday, after your mediumship is more developed, you may attend the Arthur Findlay College in England where I trained."

Eventually, five or six people entered the room and sat in the circle. A young woman named Kate was seated to my left. Following an extended meditation, the teacher asked, "James, did anything occur for you during the meditation?"

My nervousness and shyness urged me to say, "No." I disliked the spotlight on me in a group. But, I thought, *I didn't come all this way to sit quietly.* I *had* seen something, so I spoke.

"I saw a man standing behind this young woman on my left. He's actually still there. He's behind her left shoulder," I said. "He has a big round stomach. He looks like he's in his late sixties. His white hair is thinning and he's wearing a grey wool suit with a vest. It looks like an old-style tweed suit. He makes me feel like he has something to do with music and could have even been a bandleader. He says he wants Kate to, 'keep going with her music,' " I said.

I waited for someone to say something, but everyone was silent, which surprised me. I quickly and distinctly got the message that communication with the deceased was very sacred. It was not an event for applause and fanfare. No one said a thing—there was no feedback. The teacher moved on to the next person. At the end of the meeting, she invited me to attend meetings with her, at her home in Boston. She explained that a group of mediums got together every other Wednesday. I gladly accepted. I was relieved. I knew I'd learn a few things from this woman. *Maybe I'll be able to make sense of everything that's happened to me,* I thought.

As I left the meeting, Kate, who had been seated on my left, said she had been a mediumship student for a few years. She encouraged me to attend the meetings each month in Boston.

"By the way, I had an uncle who had a connection with music. And music has always been a big part of my life," Kate said.

For the next few years, I traveled from Connecticut to Massachusetts twice a month to attend classes at the teacher's home with a group of mediums. Each session began with an inspirational talk, followed by each medium giving a reading to another. Feedback was given and each student was encouraged to continue practicing doing readings during the week. One of the experienced students told me that developing mediumship was not a quick process.

"Give it at least ten years," he said. *Wow, that's longer than it took me to earn my doctorate degree,* I thought. But I wasn't discouraged. I was finally ready for some long and serious work.

30

Angel in the Classroom

Angels: a messenger in Christian, Islamic and Judaic tradition

It was a very special evening. My teacher's teacher was visiting from London. She was an internationally known medium and spiritual teacher who I looked forward to meeting. I sat quietly listening while she explained the difference between psychic readings and mediumistic readings and how the energy differed between the two. It was exciting, comforting, and validating to hear someone speak about phenomena I had experienced all my life. I understood everything she was saying. She explained things in a way that I was able to finally make sense of experiences I had had since childhood. For example, she helped me to understand the feeling in my body when I received psychic information, that my *knowing* things was natural, that seeing apparitions in various ways was part of being a medium, and that hearing the sounds and voices of spirits was definitely part of the ability. I was grateful for the opportunity to learn from her.

My mediumship was moving forward. Much of the anxiety that had accompanied my apparitions and visitations had been greatly reduced—not totally, but it was getting better. I was connected with a group of mediums, people who had lived through similar experiences, and I felt a kinship with them.

One particular Wednesday night, the seminar began no differently than any other, except that Bonnie, a well-known guest medium from London, was leading the discussion. The room was dimly lit. Statues of deities representing the great religions of the world adorned the table in the center of the room. Bright tapestries hung from the walls.

My attention was drawn to a gentleman seated in the middle of the room. I had not seen this man at any of our previous meetings. He leaned forward in his chair, listening attentively to every word the British medium spoke. I continued to be drawn to this fellow. As I watched him, I saw what appeared to be an angel standing directly behind him. I looked away and then back again—it was definitely an angel.

The figure I saw was about six feet tall and wore a long white robe. I detected blonde hair but couldn't determine whether the angel vision was male or female. Oddly enough, it felt as if it were both male and female. I didn't see the traditional wings shown in paintings, but there was little doubt that I was looking at an angel figure, standing about thirty feet from me, directly behind this older man. It was stooping down and bent forward from the waist. The angel's arms were positioned at the middle of the man's back. Up to this point in my life, I had not believed that angels actually existed. Now I believed. I decided not to mention what I had seen in fear that no one would have believed me—even other mediums.

The following month, I arrived early to the mediumship class and was waiting outside on the deck with two other mediums.

"Does anyone know the older man who was here last month? A guy, maybe in his late seventies?" I asked.

"Sure. That's Tom," Sarah replied. "He doesn't show up all the time. He's still recovering from a heart attack and a back problem that he suffered a couple of months ago."

As I had just met these two people, I wasn't comfortable sharing what I had seen the previous month. I had become convinced that this man was receiving healing from the angel that night. The angel's arms were positioned at Tom's upper back, at the heart level. My explanation sounded far-fetched, but then again, so did seeing an *angel*.

The next day, Lynnie asked me if I'd be kind enough to drive Bonnie, the British medium, to the local Spiritualist Church where she was scheduled to give mediumistic readings to the congregation. Before we left for the church, she gave me a brief psychic reading.

"I see you writing a book," Bonnie told me.

"Well, I've been thinking about writing a memoir based upon all the clairvoyant experiences I've had in my life. Is that what you see?" I asked.

"No. You may well write a memoir, but I also see a book based on spirituality. I also see you becoming a very good medium," she said.

The following morning, Bonnie taught a class on mediumship to about thirty of us who were beginner students. At one point, she motioned to me to come up on the stage with her. I was taken by surprise. It happened so quickly that I didn't have time to become nervous. I couldn't imagine why she wanted me up on stage with her.

"James, give the room a reading," Bonnie said. I began to laugh.

"What?" I asked. She placed her hand at the middle of my back. Immediately my anxiety subsided.

"I'm seeing a young man dressed in a black jumpsuit. It looks like a Japanese outfit, but the man is American. He's showing me how to do karate kicks. He died very young."

"Does anyone know this young man?" Bonnie asked the audience. A woman to the right side of the room raised her hand.

"You just did your first platform reading." Bonnie smiled at me.

I took my seat. I was supercharged with energy. I wasn't sure whether the energy was from my nervousness, from Bonnie's hand on my back, or from spirit. Maybe it was all of the above.

Later, I learned that this woman had taught mediumship, not only in Great Britain, but all over the world—she reminded me that back in those days, there were no websites, advertising, or social media for people like us.

"Spirit will place the medium where they are needed," Bonnie said.

My teachers had confidence in me...I lacked confidence. I was my own worst enemy. I continually tried to convince myself that communicating with dead people was not possible. On the rare day I accepted the possibility, I argued with myself that it was contrary to the laws of nature and religion. I was worried that my friends and co-workers would think I was crazy. I always had an excuse not to believe. The list was endless.

Lynnie made arrangements for me to give mediumship readings on a regular basis. I would sit at home in Connecticut and give readings to people all over America by phone.

"I'll send you the first name and phone number of the people I want you to give a reading for. I'm not giving you any last names—therefore the client will know you could not have searched the Internet for any personal information. You will have to provide at least five pieces of evidence to prove you have connected with their deceased loved one. Send the client a text message and let them know when you'll be calling," Lynnie said.

I was already nervous. I could not imagine having to call a perfect stranger and giving them a reading over the phone.

"Your clients won't be charged for the readings. They've agreed instead to call me to provide me with feedback about your reading," Lynnie said.

My homework was to give mediumistic readings to people I'd never met, never spoken to and never laid eyes on. How could this be possible? I knew I was able to give a pretty good reading if the person were sitting across the table from me, but on the telephone?

Lynnie explained that my readings had to be done by telephone to ensure I wouldn't receive any visual cues from the person. Later, I learned that this was the method used by researchers to study the abilities of mediums. If a student can call a complete stranger on the phone and give them an evidential reading, that's pretty good proof that the student has some mediumistic abilities.

The information I delivered had to be mediumistic, not psychic. This meant that I had to be connected to the energy of the deceased and not to the energy of the client. My readings had to provide enough evidence from the deceased spirit to convince the client that I had made contact with the deceased. Part of my training was to be able to distinguish whether the evidence I received came from the psychic realm or directly from the deceased spirit. I was ready. I knew the difference between a psychic connection and a mediumistic connection. The two felt very different.

During one call, I mentioned to the female client that she had recently had knee surgery. In another, I gave the client the month she was born. In still another, I told a woman that she had a small white dog sitting on her lap. Amazed as I was to provide such specific information to perfect strangers, none of it was useful to my mediumship training. I was receiving the information psychically, not mediumistically.

Lynnie reminded me, "If you're serious about being a medium, it would be best to leave the psychic realm alone for now. You need only to give the client information that comes directly from their loved one in spirit."

She was right. I didn't receive a report card, but if I had, the identification of the client's pet, birth month, or health issues would have earned me a failing grade. It was psychic information, not mediumistic information. These mistakes nevertheless allowed me to hone my ability to feel the difference between psychic energy and mediumistic energy.

"You should know whether the spirit was male or female, the cause of death, their relationship to the client, the age of passing, names, dates, where they lived, hobbies, profession, and other facts about their personality that come into your clairvoyant awareness," Lynnie instructed.

The primary purpose to connect with Spirit was to prove to the client the continuity of life after death. Mediumship readings are spiritual and healing in nature. In my view, my ability to give readings is a stepping-stone in my personal spiritual development. It's important for a medium to remember this and not view their ability as the end point of their development. Mediumship is not a parlor game or a means to become rich and famous. It's a spiritual activity that helps the medium to "Know Thyself."

During the next few years, I continued with what I referred to as My Mediumship Practicum. The best method to strengthen my ability proved to be by giving as many readings as possible. I phoned people all over the world and gave them readings. Some readings were very good, but some were not. However, on each occasion, I managed to connect with the deceased. My teacher and other medium friends were kind enough to refer clients to me so I could continue to practice. This had been the method of development used for my teacher, Lynnie, and her teacher, Bonnie. The lineage of the training methods used can by traced back to Gordon Higginson and even to others before him. At the time, I didn't know that some of the people I had called to read for were psychic mediums themselves. I suppose if another medium thought I was a medium, then maybe I was?

31

Belief and Confidence

"Because thou hast seen me, thou hast believed."

—John 20:29

What's keeping me from believing? That's the question I struggled with for a long time. Despite the fact that I had been giving readings each week, it was difficult to comprehend how communication with the dead was actually possible. On the days I accepted my ability, I wondered if I were just a psychic picking up evidence from the client. On other days, I wished that my readings would be terrible and that my evidence would be wrong. That way, I could say to myself, *See, there's no such thing as mediumship.* I was brutal with myself. Crazy—I know!

I do believe that I'm psychic. I accept that. I've had this ability since childhood. I don't totally understand it, but I accept it. I also accept that I have an ability to see auras or energy fields around people. The colors I see have a specific meaning for me. And, where colors are located around a person's chakras gives me information about them. "Chakra" is a Sanskrit word that translates as "wheel." In Hinduism and Buddhism, chakras are believed to be focal points of energy. This ability helps me when doing psychic readings. I receive mental, emotional, and physical information about a person. But this is psychic information and a far cry from communicating with the dead.

I occasionally see apparitions. Sometimes they appear as cloudy figures, other times I see them as clearly as I see myself in the mirror. This too, I think, is a psychic ability. The Irish call it second sight. In Hinduism, it's referred to as the third eye, or the chakra in the region of the forehead. My casual study of the world's great religions was, and continues to be, helpful in my understanding of spiritualism and mediumship. I've come to understand the common spiritual thread holding everyone together. But to actually communicate with someone who is dead, that is a whole different category. It took me a long time to really believe it's possible, even after receiving evidence and positive feedback. Most mediums need a lot of proof before they believe in anything metaphysical. We can be a very critical group. Sometimes, I was able to provide evidence about the deceased that was correct but evidence that my client was not aware of. Then, after the client conducted some family research, they were able to substantiate that evidence. On occasions when this happened, I knew unequivocally that mediumship was absolutely authentic. I was being given information from Spirit that the client was not aware of. So, I definitely could not have been receiving psychic information from that client because they didn't even know about it. The information had to come from Spirit.

I give readings in a slightly different state of consciousness. I'm not asleep...far from it. I'm supercharged. Years ago, I heard the phrase, "in the power." I guess that's as good an explanation as any. It's probably a light trance or something similar to the alpha and theta brain wave states we all reach during sleep. I am aware that I'm not in my normal daytime state of mind. In fact, I've shifted my awareness away from this world. Often, I don't remember the facts of my readings. If I didn't take notes, I'd probably forget that I'm a medium altogether!

How the medium gets into that state of preparation, I'm not really sure. I've heard mediums mention everything from by moving into the heart chakra, moving away from the mind of logic and cognitive thought, doing yogic exercise, listening to soothing music...even by listening to loud rock 'n' roll. Every medium is different but we all work with energy. There is no cookie-cutter way for your soul to behave. Spirit will work with you. It's not about the medium, it's about

Belief and Confidence

the spirit of the deceased and the person who wishes to hear from them (the "sitter").

Spirit energy from the deceased usually enters my clairvoyant vision about a half hour before I make my phone calls. I always try to have the spirit wait until I'm speaking with the client, but oftentimes the spirit is very eager. Then, I start writing everything down. I wasn't taught to do this...it's what felt natural to me. I keep notes of every reading I've ever given. That way, I'm left with written proof—a record—that I've communicated with the dead. I don't actually read my notes when I give the reading as that would pull me away from the spirit and send me back into my mind. If you're in your mind, you're thinking, and not connected to Spirit. When I give my reading it's my "time out of mind," so to speak.

When I receive information from the deceased, I often draw pictures. As I mentioned earlier, I wasn't taught to do this. It just happened that way. I am by no means an artist. Some gifted medium friends are able to draw perfect portraits of the deceased while communicating with them—not me. I wish I could because I see the deceased quite clearly. I've been told that Spirit might help me draw, but that hasn't happened yet. The act of drawing, even stick figures, somehow provides me with information about the client.

I became very upset one day when a client called my teacher to give feedback about my reading.

"James is a great psychic, but I'm not sure about his mediumistic ability," the woman had reported.

During the call, this client did not or would not accept the information I provided to her about her mother. Even after I went to my psychic awareness and told her she was holding a small white dog in her lap—she just couldn't understand how I *knew* and she was not ready to accept certain mediumistic information concerning her mother. These are the kind of responses that mediums are sometimes confronted with.

I wanted to be an accomplished medium, not a psychic. I wanted every reading to be perfect. Evidential mediumship is the work of a healer, and I had begun to see myself as a healer. I kept reminding myself that I was given the ability *to see* the dead. There had to be a reason for this. I was not going to give up.

"When an opera singer performs a difficult Mozart aria, they're still an opera singer, even on evenings they don't hit every note perfectly," Lynnie would remind me.

Many of my early readings were pretty good. They had profound healing effects on clients who had lost loved ones. These were humbling experiences. My ability helped families in ways I was not aware of. However, especially in the beginning, there were times when the readings didn't happen as smoothly or when the evidence was not crystal clear.

I wanted to build upon my own spiritual energy in order to become a better medium. Slowly, my doubts and reluctance to embrace my ability began to disappear. I accepted in my heart that I was a psychic and a medium. And, that I was able to help people in their time of grief. I embraced my paranormal experiences as a part of who I am. I was out of the closet—or at least, the door was ajar.

32

A Second Near-Death Experience

*"My grandmother walked toward me. But how? I wondered.
She died before I was born."*

—J. Deary, Emergency Room, 2012

"Sallie! Take me to the hospital!"

The emergency room was four miles from our condo. Sallie got us there in less than five minutes. By the time I was put into the wheelchair, I was feeling a little better. I didn't know what was wrong with me. I did know that my body felt different than it ever had before. I had zero pain. Quite the opposite, I was close to feeling nothing. It comforted me to know I was in a place where I'd be taken care of.

"Possible heart attack," a nurse shouted.

Her comment should have scared me to death, but it didn't. Quite the contrary, I had the distinct feeling that everything was going to be all right. In hindsight, I should have been scared to death, because Sallie was. She had just lost both parents and did not want to lose her husband.

"The nurse said that your vital signs look good. The troponin blood test was negative—meaning no heart attack—but the doctors want to repeat it. You'll be here overnight," Sallie said.

I sat in a wheelchair in the patient section of the cardiac care unit, waiting for a bed. Sallie was next to me. As we spoke, I was overtaken by a sensation of calm and serenity. I think I was slipping away.

"Your face is turning grey. I'm going to get the nurse!" Sallie shouted, and ran to the nursing station. As I waited, a woman entered the room from the door on my right and rushed directly toward me.

I assumed she was the nurse although she was wearing a skirt and blouse. She moved very fast for a woman her size. She was my grandmother! My father's mother was standing in front of me. How was this possible? My grandmother died before I was born. After that moment, I remember nothing.

When I think back on that experience, I believe that it was at that moment that I suffered my heart attack. It felt like I had peacefully slipped away. It was incredibly easy. Somehow, I was certain that whatever happened would be okay. My death or near-death experience was quite peaceful—no fear. In fact, as strange as it may seem, it was a welcomed experience. Sometime later, I woke to the sound of Sallie's voice.

"Your troponin blood test was positive this time. You had a heart attack. They've scheduled you for heart surgery in a few hours," she said.

I remember the nurse handing me a lot of forms to sign. She said if the surgeon wasn't able to place the stent in my artery, he would immediately begin open-heart surgery. Her voice carried a "you're in a life-or-death situation" tone.

Hours passed. I remember lying on a narrow operating table. The stainless steel was cold against my back and legs. Bright overhead lights caused me to look away. Velcro restraints were fastened around my wrists and ankles. There was a large-screen monitor above my head. Men dressed in white with mask-covered faces were all around me. Suddenly, I felt a severe pain in my chest. I was conscious enough to be aware that a long piece of metal was being snaked up from my right groin into my heart. The pain was severe. I was scared. I squirmed on the table.

"Don't move!" one surgeon screamed.

"Anesthesia!" another one yelled.

My next memory was in the post-op recovery room.

"You were 99% blocked in your LAD. We call that artery the 'widow-maker.' You've had a heart attack, but now your blood flow is 100%," the surgeon reassured me.

I was familiar with the term widow-maker. I knew that referred to a blockage in the largest coronary artery in the heart. Needless to say, I felt extremely lucky to be alive.

A Second Near-Death Experience

At that moment, my surgeon put his hand on my chest. He whispered a few words like he was praying. At that point, I accepted all the help I could get.

The next day, Sallie visited me in the cardiac care unit.

"Sallie, I saw my grandmother yesterday. My father's mother," I said.

"Seriously? What did she say?"

"Nothing. She walked right up to me when you went to get the nurse," I said.

"She probably showed up to save your life. You were gray. I think you were dying," Sallie said.

I had had the same thought. I seldom, if ever, think about my father's mother. She had passed away years before I was born. I was aware that she and I shared the same genetic blood problem called hemochromatosis, or iron-overload disease. It's sometimes called The Irish Curse. The only treatment is to remove a half-liter of blood every seven weeks. That treatment was not known back in my grandmother's era. Subsequently, she died of liver problems. For this reason, I never forget to have my blood removed every seven weeks.

On the third morning, Sallie arrived at the hospital around 10:00 a.m. She carried a book written by my surgeon.

"You know, you were really lucky having that doctor as your surgeon. He's very well known," she said.

"I guess somebody up there was watching over me," I smiled.

"I've been reading your surgeon's book. He's also a minister," she said.

"Really?"

"He wrote about an experience he had a few years ago when performing a heart procedure on a man. The patient died on the operating table."

"Just what I needed to hear," I joked.

"The doctors shocked the man's chest for quite a while without success. They did everything they could, then pronounced the guy legally dead," Sallie said.

"I'm glad I didn't know this a few days ago," I quipped.

"No. Listen to this...Right after leaving the operating room, your surgeon 'heard a voice' tell him, 'Go back in and shock that man again.' His surgical team had already left. Ten minutes had passed, so he went back in by himself and shocked the guy's chest. The dead man came back to life! Four physicians had pronounced him dead ten minutes earlier! This was a life-changing event for your surgeon and why he became a minister," Sallie said.

"Wow! Now I understand why he put his hand on my chest and prayed," I said.

I was scheduled for discharge the next morning. Sallie arrived early. We were happy to go home together after everything that had happened. Sallie sat next to me as we waited—hospital rules were that I had to be wheeled out of the hospital by a nurse.

"Do you remember Angela, my night nurse?" I asked Sallie.

"Yes, she's the one who has a long commute to the hospital each day," Sallie said.

"Well, I've seen a young male spirit with her a few times," I said.

"Did you tell her?" Sallie asked.

"No. I'm her patient. Besides, my teacher told me not to give readings to people who haven't asked for them," I said.

At 10:00 a.m., Angela brought me a pile of discharge papers to sign.

"I didn't think I'd see you again," I said.

"Yes, you're stuck with me again. They assigned me a double shift at the last minute. I was supposed to be at home by now. Sign these papers and I'll be back in a few minutes," she said.

"Sallie, I still see the male spirit with her. I'm feeling it's her brother," I said. Just then, Angela returned.

"Look, I don't know what your beliefs are concerning the afterlife, but my husband is a medium. He sees a man with you," Sallie said to the nurse. I don't know who was more surprised, the nurse or me. Instinctively, I began to speak.

A Second Near-Death Experience

"Did you lose a brother? Did he pass in his early forties?" I asked. The nurse looked stunned as she came and stood by my wheelchair.

"Yes," she replied. I saw tears in her eyes.

"He was your older brother, wasn't he?" I asked.

"Yes. How did you know that?" she asked.

"He's always walking in front of you like he's leading the way for you. It's like he's helping you with your work here in the hospital. Maybe he's even helping me get discharged," I said.

"Yes, he helped me do everything. He always led the way for me," she said.

"He's quite a preppy dresser, isn't he?" I asked.

"Yes, he certainly was," she smiled. "I was his little sister," she said.

"I know," I replied.

I continued to provide her with evidence for nearly a half hour. She asked a wide variety of questions about mediumship and how communication with the deceased was possible. I answered her to the best of my ability. I thanked her for allowing me to channel her brother and reminded her that he was always with her, helping to lead the way. She wished me well in my recovery.

"I believe that Spirit arranged for Angela to work a double shift so she'd be here to receive the message from her brother. She wasn't supposed to be working this morning," Sallie said.

Every day for the next few weeks I returned to the hospital for physical therapy. I looked forward to running into Angela again, but I never did.

33

Holy Cannoli, I Can Hear

Clairaudience: the power of hearing something not present to the ear but having objective reality

Death had spared me for a second time. I couldn't remember anything about drowning at age two, but the heart-attack experience was with me forever. I was happy to be alive and looking forward to 2013. I was on borrowed time, but aren't we all? I always had a genuine appreciation for life but after my near-death experience, I'm grateful for every minute of every day. The vast majority of men do not survive the type of heart attack I had. There's a reason why it's called the widow-maker.

A few weeks later, the severity of what I had been through finally hit me. I came to the sobering realization that I had almost died. Actually, I really do think that for a brief moment, I did die. It happened the instant I saw my grandmother walking into my hospital room. It had not been a visitation as happened with my spirit guide years ago. My paternal grandmother, whom I had never met, was there with me in the room. I have little doubt that she saved my life that day. I'd always felt a strong connection with her from the time I learned that she passed away from the same inherited genetic blood condition that I have—that Irish Curse, hemochromatosis.

After coming to grips with the seriousness of what had happened, I became frightened. Ironically, when the heart attack was happening, I wasn't afraid. It was a peaceful experience, and I was accepting of it. In a strange way, dying felt like something to look forward to. But after,

I was scared to death of death. I asked myself over and over again why I had been spared a second time. There must be a reason.

"Clairaudience... the ability to hear, using our spiritual senses."

—Eileen Davies, Mastery of Mediumship, 2020

Meatballs and spaghetti! Who could refuse? One evening, there was a knock at the front door of our Florida condo. Our next-door neighbor, Roxy, invited Sallie and me to the Catholic Church's annual spaghetti dinner. What better way to get my mind off my ordeal than a meatball and spaghetti dinner?

Roxy's brother was a bakery chef. Cannoli was his specialty. Actually, he made cannoli for nearly all the restaurants in the Italian North End of Boston. Once every year, he flew down to south Florida to cook spaghetti and meatballs for the woman's contingent of the Knights of Columbus. The event was a huge fundraiser for the Catholic Church. More importantly, everyone was well aware that a famous Italian baker from Boston would be in town to make cannoli for dessert.

Sallie bought five tickets for the spaghetti dinner. The idea was to support Roxy, who was the chairperson of the event.

We arrived at the church basement around 6:00 p.m. and handed two entrance tickets to the woman seated at a table near the front door of the church basement.

"Do you want to buy some raffle tickets?" the woman asked Sallie.

"Sal, that's a waste of money. When was the last time you won anything?" I whispered.

"It's for charity," Sallie reminded me.

I reached into my pocket to pay while the woman unraveled a handful of blue raffle tickets from a large wooden spool on the table.

She kept turning the spool around and around before stopping to tear off a large handful of tickets.

"How many tickets did you ask her for?" I asked. Sallie didn't answer. To my surprise, the instant she put the tickets into my hand, I felt a nervous electric sensation move over my body. Without any conscious thought, I turned toward Sallie and blurted out in a loud voice, "I'm not going up on that stage to get the money. You'll have to go up by yourself." Sallie looked at me like I was crazy.

"What? What are you talking about?" Sallie asked. I had no clue why I said what I said. It was as if my voice spoke by itself.

"You're going to win the grand prize...And, I don't want to get up on stage," I reiterated.

My body tingled. I had the same invigorating nervous feeling I get when a deceased spirit comes near. *Maybe a spirit caused me to say those words*, I thought to myself. I couldn't explain it and didn't want to try. I was too hungry.

We sat down to a large plate of spaghetti and meatballs. I went to the dessert table and took a few cannoli, knowing they would disappear if I waited. The blue raffle tickets sat front of us on the table. After dinner, the band began to play sixties dance music.

"I'm ready to leave. I'm not interested in listening to oldies music," Sallie said.

"Me either, but you are going to win some money tonight," I reassured Sallie.

"Sure I am," she said jokingly.

The dance floor quickly filled with older retired people having fun. It was like an Italian wedding—without the bride and groom. During intermission, a large man stood up to the microphone.

"Who's ready to win some cash?" he shouted with a Brooklyn accent. I turned to Sallie and smiled. I was reminded of being back in New York City.

"I'll draw three tickets from the paper bag. I'm your 'Brooklyn bagman,'" he joked.

"You know, my mother, Anna Mae, liked to gamble at church outings," Sallie whispered.

169

"No kidding!" I replied.

"First ticket wins a free lunch at Carmine's Restaurant," the Brooklyn man shouted.

"I knew your mom liked the lottery," I said.

"Second ticket wins a free dinner at Carmine's," the man yelled.

"Mom was very lucky. She won quite a few times," Sallie said.

"Third ticket wins all the cash!" the man screamed.

The first and second prizes were awarded. Everyone waited patiently. The main event was coming next. Someone would go home with all the cash.

A hush fell over the audience as the man began the grand drawing. The brass section of the band played "Charge!" the way it's played at baseball games. Everyone shouted "Charge!" in unison. The man beckoned to a little girl in the audience to come up front and pick the winning number from the paper bag.

"Reach in little girl and give me a ticket...just one!" the man instructed.

We listened as the man shouted six numbers into the microphone, his heavy Brooklyn accent making the speaker system squeal with feedback as he called out each number. He began to repeat the winning numbers a second time when Sallie's face took on a look of surprise and disbelief.

She smiled, wide-eyed, at me across the table. She stood and walked across the dance floor toward the stage. Her arm was raised and she was shaking the small blue ticket in her hand. The man from Brooklyn handed her a white envelope thick with cash.

"I'm your Brooklyn bag-man, Sweetie," he said. The audience laughed, applauded, and whistled all at the same time.

The envelope was stuffed with fifty-dollar bills. Sallie could hardly keep the cash from falling all over the table. I was excited for her—and excited because I had just had an experience unlike anything before. I had actually *heard a voice telling me* that Sallie would win the grand prize.

"I still can't believe we won. You know, it was my mother who told you that I would win the grand prize," Sallie said.

"You could be right. Maybe she wanted to send you a message that she's still with you," I said. Sallie counted out half of the cash and walked over to the table where Roxy, the chairperson, was seated.

"I want to donate this money to the church. It's from my mother, Anna Mae."

34

Spirits in the Storm

"They need our help—they're in trouble."

—Chris, South Florida, October 1, 2015

Circle was a wonderful way for mediums to practice their skills. I co-hosted a Circle in Florida with Michele for three years. Seven mediums gathered in my living room twice a month to give mediumistic readings to one another. It never ceased to amaze me how many deceased friends and family members presented themselves during that time.

Our October 1st, 2015, Circle meeting began no differently than any other. Earlier in the week, I had considered cancelling the Circle due to the threat of Hurricane Joaquin that was bearing down on South Florida. All week long, the National Weather Service had been unable to determine whether the hurricane would travel westward into the Florida coast or track eastward out to sea.

As the hurricane had moved far enough away and remained out into the Atlantic, we went forth with our meeting. As we began the Circle that evening, we offered a prayer for anyone who might find themselves in the path of Joaquin. All of us had lived in Florida long enough to know all too well what could happen during a Category 5 hurricane.

The seven of us were seated in my living room, ready to begin our meditation.

"Where's Chris?" I asked.

"I saw him in the parking lot. He said he wanted to take a look at the ocean before coming upstairs—it's like a meditation for Chris," Michele said.

A few minutes later, Chris joined us. He was noticeably preoccupied. "Chris, what's the matter?" I asked.

He didn't answer. He quietly took a seat on my left. He sat, gazing out into space. This behavior was not unusual. Mediums usually require a shift in their awareness before giving a reading. However, something felt very different to me. All the mediums turned toward Chris. We thought he was about to begin a reading for one of us. Instead, as he sat there, a look of panic crossed his face.

"Are you okay, Chris?" I repeated.

"They need our help—NOW!" Chris shouted. Chris seemed desperate—yet he looked like he was in a trance.

"Jim, can you *see* them?" Chris asked.

Chris knew I had been able to see Spirit from a young age. He was staring toward the front entrance of my condo. I followed Chris's gaze and turned toward the front door. Suddenly, about ten feet away, I saw eight to ten cloudy-looking ghost-like figures standing in my living room where Chris's gaze was focused. I could not believe my eyes. I was in a state of electric shock. One of the men stood out very clearly to me. He was a full-body apparition dressed in military clothing.

"I think they're sailors," Chris said.

"They are," I responded quickly. Somehow both of us knew.

"I can see one of the men very clearly. He's wearing a dark-blue double-breasted jacket with gold buttons. He looks like a ship's officer," I said.

"They need our help—they're in trouble!" Chris shouted again. Still in a trance-like state, he was pleading with us to try to help. Chris's face showed extreme anguish, as if he were witnessing an event in real time. Often a medium will experience some of the same physical and emotional sensations of the spirit he's connected with—but this was even more dramatic, as if the both of us were experiencing an actual tragic event.

"I *feel* like these people drowned." I said. I wanted to try to explain what was happening for my own peace of mind. "I'm sure hundreds of people have drowned out there in the Atlantic at one time or another. Maybe we're psychically witnessing an event that happened years ago," I continued, attempting to reassure the group and myself.

"I'm not so sure. I'm feeling a sense of urgency. Like I should be doing something to help—right now!" Chris spoke firmly in a raised voice. The other members of the Circle continued to listen intently. Only Chris and I saw the apparition.

"I saw an officer in spirit standing by my front door. He wasn't alone. He was with a group of other men. The man I saw clearly was a middle-aged guy, black hair, and wearing a brass-buttoned military-type jacket. I couldn't see the other men well enough to describe them," I said.

"One of them was Black," Chris said.

"Really! You saw them too?" I asked.

"Only one clearly. I only saw a Black man," Chris replied.

"It's always difficult to explain what exactly is going on when there's no evidence to rely upon. You two could have witnessed an energy imprint of an event that happened years ago. It's hard to say," Michele offered.

In unison, Chris and I shouted, "No!" We somehow knew this was not an imprint of something from the past.

Many times, our Circle had connected with spirits that no one could identify. And, occasionally, one of us would see a spirit near our Circle that no one could identify. Because we had been trained as evidential mediums, we would say a prayer for the unidentified spirit visitor, and then move on. This was exactly what we did that evening. No one in the Circle could identify the two spirits who had not directly communicated with Chris or myself. There was no evidence to be provided, so we moved on.

The next morning, my cellphone was flooded with text messages from members of the Circle that made little sense to me. Then my phone rang.

"Did you see the news this morning?" Michele asked.

"No. I just got up," I replied.

"Turn it on, now," she ordered. I couldn't believe it—every network reported some version of the following:

"The cargo ship *El Faro* was lost at sea last night. It's not known if there were any survivors. The ship was traveling from Jacksonville,

Florida to Puerto Rico when it encountered hurricane Joaquin. NOAA reported that the ship most likely encountered 155 mph winds and fifty-foot seas. There were thirty-three crew members aboard," the reporter said.

Oh my god. My heart sank in my chest. I could not wrap my mind around what I thought had happened the night before. Had some of the members of the *El Faro* crew actually shown themselves in my living room last night? How on Earth was that possible?

Our spirit visitors were not imprints from accidents that had happened years ago. Those sailors had drowned last night while we sat in our Circle. Their cargo ship, *El Faro*, sank during the hurricane.

Following Michele's phone call, I was overcome with sadness and disbelief. Chris and I had witnessed a tragedy by means of our clairvoyant ability.

My clear vision of the uniformed sailor remained fresh in my memory for quite some time. The evening news reported that the Coast Guard had initiated a search with ships and planes. Based upon what Chris and I saw and felt the night before, I knew there would be no survivors. My heart broke for the families of the crew, of which many were from Florida. For days, the news covered the rescue efforts. The families continued to have hope.

During that time, I searched the Internet for photos and names of the crewmembers. I wanted to be wrong. More than anything, I didn't want our clairvoyant vision to have been true. I hoped and prayed that the interpretation of our vision was incorrect. I prayed that the sailors would be found adrift in a lifeboat. But deep down inside, I *knew* what the outcome would be. It was a very difficult time for me. *Was this the life of a medium and psychic? Do I want a life with this kind of heartache?* I asked myself.

Months later, an investigative report about the sinking of the *El Faro* was published. All thirty-three members of the crew had disappeared. The cargo ship's black box had finally been retrieved and showed that the ship itself had been experiencing mechanical trouble just as Chris shouted that evening. The real trouble began when the ship lost engine power and was at the mercy of the storm. I couldn't substantiate the exact time the crew drowned, but it was within minutes of our

Circle meeting that Thursday evening. The sailors must have showed up in my living room the instant they passed away that night.

The crew was at the mercy of up to fifty-foot seas and up to 155 mph winds! They were definitely "in trouble"—Chris's words echoed in my head.

A year later, the news media released a report with photos and biographies of the crew. I will never forget scrolling through the photos of the thirty-three crewmembers. The pictures and biographies brought each person to life and tears to my eyes.

One photo showed the African American sailor that Chris had seen. Then, on the last page of the report was the photo I'll never forget: in his double-breasted blue dress uniform with gold buttons was the officer I had seen standing in my living room that evening.

Sometime later, I shared this story with the internationally famous medium, Mavis Pittilla. I was looking for some kind of explanation for how and why this could happen during our Circle and in real time.

"You mediums were like bright headlights in the darkness of night for those deceased spirits," Mavis replied.

35

SPIRITS OF SEDONA

"Eight feet away from my bed stood the full body apparition of an American Indian."

—J. Deary, Sedona, 2015

I have never considered myself a New Age person. I'd usually joke that being a medium was more like an Old Age ability. I never had a great deal of interest to travel the world in search of spiritual sites—it just wasn't my cup of tea. Sedona, Arizona was a whole different situation. I had heard it was a beautiful western town with red rock canyons not too far from the Grand Canyon. Later, I learned that tourists flock to Sedona for spiritual reasons as well as wanting to enjoy its beautifully surreal landscape.

Sallie and I really enjoyed the southwest desert—in fact, we were married in the California desert years earlier. I had learned to appreciate the quiet of the desert during the years I worked off the coast of Africa in the Canary Islands. There was a large sand dune desert on the south end of Gran Canaria. They say that geographically, it had once been connected to the Sahara Desert. Today, it's separated from the Sahara by about fifty miles of Atlantic Ocean. The deep sand dunes absorb all the sounds of civilization—it's an incredibly quiet and peaceful place.

I had never heard of the term "vortex" prior to our Sedona visit. A friend there explained that a vortex was a concentrated area of energy, not unlike that found at the Sphinx, Stonehenge, and Machu Picchu, to name a few locations. I have to admit I still had no idea what a vortex was, even after hearing the explanation. It didn't make much sense to me, and no one could show me any evidence to support the existence of this vortex energy. I could accept that energy was connected to human beings, but it was a stretch for me to believe energy was connected to certain locations on the planet. I've since changed my mind.

We reserved a room at a resort in Sedona's Boynton Canyon area. A friend from my Circle had recommended the resort because it had a beautiful meditation center on the property. The 120-mile drive from Phoenix took longer than I had anticipated. It was a slow climb past cactus and sagebrush up to an elevation of 4400 feet. The hot Phoenix temperature had cooled down about twenty-five degrees by the time we reached Sedona. The terrain had also changed dramatically from sandy desert to beautiful orange-red mountains.

"When you drive through Native American land, you're in some of the most beautiful places on Earth," Sallie said.

"You're right. When you think about it, every part of America was once Indian Territory," I said. During our drive, Sallie read from the brochure she had picked up at the Phoenix Airport. It chronicled the history of Sedona.

"This part of Arizona has been Indian territory since 11,000 B.C.! The Hopi Indians have a reservation not far from here and the Apaches also lived near here. Most Indians were removed following the Civil War," Sallie continued.

"Interesting phrase, 'were removed,' " I said sarcastically.

I had trouble keeping my eyes on the road driving into Boynton Canyon. The red-rock scenery was incredible. Rock spires sat along the top of red mountains that encircled the Sedona landscape. The rocky desert reminded me of Western movies I'd seen as a kid.

Orange-red peaks were accented with horizontal white stripes. Erosion had carved spires into the tops of the mountains. As the afternoon sun drifted toward the horizon, shadows began to cover the hills with shades of blue and grey. At 4400 feet, the summer sky was bluer than blue. Sedona was a masterpiece of Mother Nature.

We checked into the resort, then headed out in our four-wheel drive vehicle to become familiar with the town. Some of the roads around the perimeter of Sedona required special low-gear vehicles capable of driving into uncharted mountain territory. Each turn in the road provided another incredible postcard view. Signposts named every mountain peak along the horizon. Bell Rock looked as if a large bell had been dropped onto the horizon and Cathedral Rock looked exactly as the name implied. I had spent many years living and working in various countries around the world but had never seen rock formations like these.

"This town should be listed as one of the wonders of the world," Sallie said.

"I know. And we've only seen half of it," I said.

That evening we saw a notice in the hotel lobby describing a tour to an energy vortex the following morning. We figured, why not? Maybe we'd come away from our vacation knowing a little more about what a vortex was all about. The hotel concierge was quick to point out that we would be traveling off-road in an open four-wheel-drive vehicle. She said it was not a ride for the squeamish who may be fearful—we'd be riding up steep mountain terrain in an open vehicle. Despite her warning, we signed up for the tour. The next morning, we met our guide, a rugged-looking middle-age character named Josey. We turned out to be his only customers that morning.

"I guess the concierge scared the hell out of everyone else," I whispered to Sallie.

"More likely that everyone else figured a vortex tour was a waste of time," Sallie said.

"I'm 'half farmer' and 'half-breed,'" Josey interrupted.

"Okay. I'll bite. What does that mean?" I asked.

"Well, on days I'm not giving vortex tours, I'm working on the farm, so, I'm half farmer. My mother is a Hopi Indian who married a white man, so I'm also a half-breed. Marrying a white man got my mother off the reservation," Josey explained.

"Reservation?" I asked.

"Yep. That's where most of the Hopi live. If you drive an hour east to Winslow then another hour north, you'll reach the Hopi Reservation. It's Indian territory," he said.

"Josey, what do you think about this energy vortex stuff? I read that it might have something to do with magnetic fields and iron deposits in the soil?" Sallie asked.

"People make of it what they want. They come here from all over the world," Josey said with a smile.

I could tell by the tone of his voice that Josey didn't want to appear naïve. To him, we were city-slickers from back east. He wasn't sure whether we believed that an energy vortex was fact or fiction. I was well aware that this man made his living driving tourists up into the mountains two or three times a week. My gut feeling told me that this Hopi Indian farmer believed there was something special about the vortex. The indigenous people had held spiritual beliefs about these mountains for thousands of years. They thought the vortex contained a special energy. Josey was clearly connected to his mother's Hopi Indian culture. I was convinced that spending time at the vortex was more than just a job for Josey.

Our Jeep veered off the primary road and onto a dusty dirt trail barely wide enough to travel. Eight-foot boulders along both sides of the trail stood as our only protection from falling into the valley below. We held tightly onto subway straps that had been bolted onto the Jeep's roll bar. I was nearly thrown out of the vehicle at the first sharp turn. I pulled tightly on my seat belt. I had to duck my head low each time the Jeep brushed by one of the large creosote bushes. Branches ripped over my right arm, drawing a little blood. The road had our constant attention. I looked at Sallie and repeated the concierge's warning, "Not for the squeamish."

When we reached the end of the dirt road, Josey pulled hard on a floor-handle to shift into the off-road transmission. He continued into unmarked territory. We were on a 30% incline. The angle was much too steep for the average off-road vehicle. Josey drove across large red rocks and mountain brush. Suddenly, the Jeep's wheels began to spin in place along a steeper incline. We were sliding backward! Quickly, he shifted back and forth between each transmission. It didn't work and we continued to slide. He took his foot off the gas and pulled hard on the hand brake. The Jeep slid, sideways this time, to a stop.

"Time to walk some," Josey grinned.

Josey sprinted up the rock-covered hill, kicking stones behind him with each stride. Sallie and I followed behind—he left us in his dust. Despite his age, we couldn't compete with him.

"There's no way a family of four could have made this trip up the mountain. Kids would have been thrown out of the Jeep," I said.

Eventually, we reached a clearing at the top of the hill. Josey joked that we must have gotten lost. He laughed while we stood, catching our breath.

"This is Bell Vortex. We can stay here as long as you want," he announced.

The view from the top was breathtaking. Sunlight bounced off the red rocks that outlined the horizon. Beneath us, lime green shrubbery was scattered across the sandy soil. The air was still. There was no wind, no birdsong, and none of the usual sounds of nature. Juniper trees were twisted in braids like giant pretzels. I asked Josey how this could happen to full-grown trees.

"They say that it's the energy up here in the vortex that caused them Juniper trees to get all twisted up," Josey said.

"Maybe it was the wind?" I asked.

"You feel any wind up here?" Josey sneered, but not unkindly.

Sallie and I walked to the far end of the clearing. It felt as if we were in a sacred silent place. I began to feel a heightened sense of awareness and then a feeling of nervous anticipation. Sallie walked to the edge of the cliff to take photos of the valley. I waited nearby, enjoying the view and the energy sensation that was washing over me. Josey sat on the ground at the other end of the clearing. After twenty minutes had passed, I motioned to Sallie that we should get going. We got back into the Jeep and began our drive down the mountain.

"It's harder, going downhill. Sometimes the wheels start to slide and the Jeep goes sideways," Josey said. Sallie and I stared wide-eyed at each other.

"Take your time, Josey," I said.

"Sallie, let me see some of those photos you took," I asked, to take my mind off the incline. She quickly pulled up the pictures she had just taken.

"What the heck is that?" Sallie yelled.

"What?" I asked.

I took the phone from Sallie's hand. One of the photos she had taken at Bell Rock Vortex was only partially "developed." Only half of the picture came out on the screen. The other half was an awkward black jagged configuration.

"Have you ever seen anything like this?" I asked Josey.

"Nope! Probably the energy," Josey said, smiling.

I'd never seen anything like it before. It looked as if something had blacked out half of the field of vision. In the years following our visit to Sedona, I've asked hundreds of people if their camera phone had ever taken a photo that looked even remotely like the one Sallie took at Bell Rock. To date, no one has, or has been able to explain it.

Was this strange photo due to some kind of vortex energy? I don't know. All I could say was that the photo was taken at the center of the Bell Rock energy vortex. A coincidence? I don't know.

The Boynton Vortex was directly across the street from our resort, but we decided not to attempt the hour-long climb up its steep rocky trail. We had had our fill of rocky climbs with Josey. Besides, we had to get up early the next morning to drive to Jerome, the old copper mining town next on our sightseeing agenda.

On our final night in Sedona, I was awakened abruptly around 3:00 a.m. My eyes had jerked open after feeling two hard slaps on my left foot—like a wooden ping-pong paddle had slapped the bottom of my foot. I immediately thought, *Why is Sallie waking me up in the middle of the night?* I pulled my left leg up to my chest to rub the bottom of my foot because the sensation continued. I had been slapped pretty hard.

I turned toward Sallie to ask what she wanted—she was sound asleep. *Did she hit my foot twice then fall back asleep?* Before I had time to figure out what had happened, I looked up and stiffened in utter surprise. About eight feet away from Sallie's side of the bed, stood the full-body apparition of a male who looked to be Native American. I was not frightened—surprised and amazed, yes—but not afraid. He was of average height, with dark hair. Though he was clearly an American Indian, he was dressed in modern clothing. He wore jeans and a blue flannel shirt. He appeared to be a man who had worked outdoors all of his life.

"Who are you? Why are you here?" I asked the man with my mind.

"I am here to watch over the mountain. It is sacred," I heard him respond.

During our communication, which lasted about five or six seconds, he told me that he had worked at the resort during his life on Earth, and that his daughter continues to work there today.

"Take the path behind your bungalow and walk up the hill. From there you will see the mountain that I watch over," he instructed.

Excited and nervous, I woke Sallie and told her what had happened. She listened and reminded me that it was the middle of the night and that we had a long day ahead of us. In a matter of minutes, we both fell back asleep.

Early the next morning, I told Sallie that I was going to take a walk up the hill behind our bungalow as the Native American had suggested.

"I have to admit that this is the first time I've ever taken orders from a spirit," I smiled at Sallie.

"Take your time. I'm going to take a shower and pack the bags," she said.

I headed outside, turned left, and continued up the path separating the bungalows from the sidewalk. I continued about another fifty yards up the hill. Reaching the end of the path, I stopped and looked around. All I saw were trees, rocks, and waist-high brush. When I turned around to head back downhill to the bungalow, there, in front of me, reaching above the pine trees was the red-rock spire of Boynton Canyon. The locals consider Boynton Canyon another vortex. The spire glowed red orange in the morning sun. I watched for a few minutes as sunlight climbed up the side of the canyon. I asked myself why this American Indian spirit wanted me to walk up the hill just to look at the Boynton Canyon spire. Not finding any answers, I shrugged my shoulders and hiked back down the hill to our bungalow.

"You get a nice look at the Boynton Canyon spire from up there on the hill," I said to Sallie.

"You also get a nice view from the porch of the hotel. Josey said there's a vortex up there near the spire but it's a rocky hike getting up there," Sallie said.

"I suppose the Indian spirit watches over the Boynton Canyon Vortex," I offered.

We drove over to the main hotel to check out. I paid the bill while Sallie spoke with the concierge about Boynton Canyon.

"So, what's it like to have the famous the Boynton Vortex right across the street from your office?" Sallie asked her.

"We get a lot of tourists who want to stay here so they can be near that vortex. A lot of hikers will spend a full day hiking up to the spire," she said.

"We visited the Bell Canyon Vortex the other day with Josey. We'll have to wait till next time to see Boynton," Sallie said.

"Well, I hope you return soon. Boynton Canyon is different from Bell Canyon. There's a lot more to Boynton Canyon than just a vortex," she said.

"What do you mean?" I asked, joining the conversation.

"Hopi Indians refer to Boynton Canyon as Kachina. They believe that the canyon is a manifestation of a sacred female spirit. Spiritually, Kachina would be similar to the Blessed Virgin or Divine Goddess. Native Americans believe that Kachina has protected all of humanity since the beginning of time," she explained.

My mind raced. My experience with the spirit apparition took on a whole new meaning. *It makes sense now*, I thought.

"The spirit I encountered is the protector of Kachina," I whispered to Sallie.

This apparition was spiritual. I slowly developed a new appreciation for the vortex. And, I had a new appreciation for communication with spirits. Mediumship is not just an evidential communication from medium to spirit to client—it is first and foremost the spiritual joining of two worlds. I had had a moment of revelation, an aha moment. Seeing the spirit of a priest or nun is always a spiritual occasion, but so is every mediumistic encounter. It's a joining of souls and the joining of two worlds.

I couldn't explain what had happened with Sallie's photo at the Bell Vortex, but I did gain a clearer understanding of my apparition with the Native American. There's something going on in Sedona for which I have no explanation.

36

An Irish Story

"Nine times Ireland has been invaded, conquered and occupied."

—*Irish Post*, October 2016

My sister died in February 2017. Losing Lenore was a devastating experience and one that I've not yet totally processed on an emotional level. She was my younger sister, my only sister. Lenore abused IV drugs as a teenager but had managed to get herself clean in her early twenties. She became a wife, mother, and businesswoman. She conquered the odds and survived to become a loving mother and friend to many. Years later, as happens with many drug addicts, she was diagnosed with hepatitis C. The medication that cured 99% of hepatitis C patients did not work for Lenore and the disease developed into metastatic liver cancer. Seven years earlier, Lenore's husband had also been diagnosed with liver cancer. He suffered through two liver transplants, both of which failed. Lenore lost her husband, then learned that she too had liver cancer. It didn't seem fair, but death never is.

As a medium, I'm confronted with death almost every day of my life. It's never been a problem. However, the grief associated with the loss of my little sister was overwhelming. Needless to say, Lenore's death was difficult not only for me but also my two brothers and our now hundred-year-old mother.

Whereas American stories usually have happy endings, Irish stories often do not. Lenore's story was an Irish story.

Lenore had always been my advocate. She resembled me both physically and emotionally and possessed many of the sensitivities that I had. My mother once told me that Lenore had cried for three days after learning my high school girlfriend left me. She took that breakup harder than I did. She was an emotionally sensitive and caring woman who felt life very deeply. Many addicts do.

It's often difficult for extremely sensitive people to navigate the complexities of life. On a psychic level, these individuals empathically absorb every emotion they come into contact with. They feel very deeply—sometimes too deeply. Lenore also possessed psychic sensitivities. She was my sounding board later in life after I had begun my mediumship training. I shared with her what I was going through during my early development as well as experiences I had had as a young man. She understood and accepted my ability, even when I became confused and doubtful of all things psychic. While I was reluctant to share my ability with anyone, Lenore sang my praises and told all her friends that her brother was a medium. She was proud of me when I wasn't feeling proud.

Two weeks after Lenore passed, my brother Tom came to visit me in Florida. One evening, while eating dinner at a local restaurant, we reminisced about Lenore.

"Do you remember the time at your house near the Connecticut River when my knees went weak in the kitchen?" I asked.

"Yes, you yelled out. You knew something had happened right there," Tom said.

"Right. Lenore whispered that she 'smelled the smoke,' " I said.

"Then, Penny told us that a woman had burned to death at that spot," Tom said.

"Lenore didn't hesitate a minute. She *knew right away* that a woman had died in a kitchen fire. It dawned on me later that Lenore and I had connected to the same spirit at the same time. I realized then and there she had psychic medium abilities," I continued.

"Have you ever seen any paranormal activity in the house since that day?" I asked Tom.

Tom, like a lot of people, wasn't really sure if I was clairvoyant or just kidding myself. I didn't expect much of a response to my question. He took a sip of wine and spun his barstool around so he was facing me.

"Yeah, I saw something once," he said. I was a bit shocked, but kept quiet and listened.

"One afternoon, I was alone in the house. I had been working upstairs on the computer. I got up and went downstairs to get a glass of water. You've been in the house. You know how you can see the living room sofa when you're walking down the staircase?"

"Sure," I said.

"I got halfway down the staircase and, sitting there on the sofa, I saw a woman. I saw her as clearly as I see you right now. She looked directly at me. It sounds scary, but I wasn't afraid," Tom said.

"My God! So you saw the lady who died in the kitchen?"

"Just that one time. She didn't speak...she just sat there," Tom said.

"I've heard that second sight ability can run in families," I said. I've met many mediums and have learned that often these abilities seem to be passed down from generation to generation. But I don't think I've ever heard about a family where almost everyone in the family has seen spirits at one time or another.

"Don't forget our mother. We grew up hearing about the time she saw the ghost-man sitting in our bedroom," Tom said.

"Yeah, I remember that story. She yelled at the ghost and told him to get out," I said laughing. A few minutes passed. The fellow sitting next to us at the bar kept looking at us like we were crazy.

"See the look on that guy's face? That's why I never mention this stuff to anyone," I whispered.

"Now that we're on the subject, I did have another experience that I never mentioned to anyone," Tom said.

"It probably won't surprise me. I've heard all kinds of stories from mediums," I said.

"I had some kind of vision," Tom began. I stopped eating to pay close attention. Seeing a spirit was a big deal for most people and a visitation is an even more rare occurrence.

"It was October 23, 1971," Tom said.

Tom had my attention. I had experienced visitations on a few occasions—they're so intense that people remember the event like it happened yesterday. Tom remembered the exact date, forty-six years earlier.

"I was awake and in bed when the room suddenly opened into what I can only describe as another dimension. There was a man dressed in gold and holding a gold staff. He stood directly above me. Off to the side was a woman with curly black hair, lying in a casket. The floor, the walls, the casket, everything was covered with red roses. I could actually smell them," Tom said.

"Did all this happen in a split-second?" I asked.

"No. It went on for longer than that," Tom said.

"Then what happened?" I asked.

"That was it, except when my ex-wife sat up in bed to ask if I smelled flowers," Tom said.

"Really? What did you tell her?" I asked.

"Nothing. I didn't tell her a thing. We were on vacation. She doesn't like scary stuff and besides, I wouldn't have known how to explain it," Tom said. I took a sip of wine.

"You know, Mom's experiences have continued into her old age," I said.

"What do you mean?" Tom asked.

"She told me that she saw a mid-eastern looking man up near the altar at the convent. I figured this was a onetime experience. But, when I questioned her, she said it had happened to her over twenty times there. She said she wanted to tell the nuns what she had seen but was worried they'd think she was a crackpot," I said.

"You think it's her imagination?" Tom asked.

"No, because the last time she was there she said she saw a different man on the left side of the altar. Her descriptions are too specific. She said he looked like a ghost that was dressed in a priest's outfit. This was a totally different vision," I said.

My family's experiences bounced around in my head. How was it that almost everyone in the family had seen spirits? Why was I the only one able to communicate with them?

"You know, the experience you had is not that different than mine," I said to Tom.

"The big difference, Jim, is that they speak to you. That would freak me out," Tom replied.

"I know. It did freak me out. It frightened me, right from the beginning," I said.

"You know that Lenore's grandson claims to have seen a man in the house," Tom said.

"I've heard that. I'm not really sure if I'd wish this ability on another family member. I'd have to think long and hard about that. It's a very big responsibility and not everyone is ready for it," I said.

37

Double Apparition

"Is this medium in Mexico talking about what I think she's talking about?"

—J. Deary, 2020

In 2020, our extended vacation to Connecticut gave Sallie and I the opportunity to more time with my ninety-seven-year-old mother. This amazing woman still spent her days raking leaves off her front lawn and coaxing squirrels down from the oak tree so she could feed them a special selection of nuts.

Retirement to Florida had brought a whole new circle of friends into our lives. We were full-time Floridians who took regular trips to Connecticut to visit friends and family.

One afternoon, Sallie and I were invited to a pool party at an old friend's estate on the Connecticut coast. We looked forward to visiting with some old acquaintances and had images of enjoying a *Great Gatsby*-type afternoon in the wealthy suburb of Westport—the same town where F. Scott Fitzgerald had actually lived for awhile.

The afternoon fun at the pool eventually moved inside where twelve or so friends gathered near the dining table for a self-serve meal. Some sat at the table while others filled their plates and returned back to the picnic table near the swimming pool.

This was the first time I had been inside the two-hundred-year-old home purchased by my friend shortly after her return from twenty years in Asia. The house interior had been redone from top to bottom but still retained its original rustic farmhouse look and feel. Unlike the modern open-floor plans of today, this home had many unique rooms designed so a mother working in the kitchen would be able to see her children in the adjacent rooms. I looked forward to a tour of the house that our hostess, Mindy, had promised after dinner. I feasted on Greek food that Mindy had personally prepared, using her mother's recipes.

Unique objects that had been accumulated during her years in Thailand, Japan, and China filled every corner of the room. My eyes darted from one interesting object to another. From where I was seated in the dining room, I was able to see into the small sitting room beyond the kitchen.

Funny. Why is that woman sitting all alone in there on the couch? I guess she's not hungry. I don't remember meeting her. Then I realized...she was not a real human being. She was wearing a black dress and looked to be in her fifties. Her jet-black hair was rolled up at the back of her head in an old-fashioned bun. She reminded me of a Greek opera star whose name escaped me at the time. She looked more real and alive than any spirit I had ever seen. As usual, I was a bit shaken by the experience. The house was very old, so I figured the woman had probably lived here many years ago.

"Come on, Jim and Sallie. Let me show you around. Everyone else has seen this place a hundred times," Mindy said. I got up from the table and whispered to Sallie, "I saw a woman sitting on the right side of that couch over there."

I had known Mindy for thirty years and felt comfortable asking her questions about her property. I thought that maybe the spirit had been a former owner of the house.

"Do you know anything about the family who lived here before you?" I asked.

"No, honey," Mindy replied in her Mississippi accent.

The three of us started down the staircase next to the sitting room. I had just begun to whisper the details of my apparition to Sallie, when all of a sudden the lights in the room began to flash on and off.

"You've got to be kidding me," I said to Sallie.

"Has this ever happened before?" I asked Mindy.

"No, honey," she said again. The lights continued to flash on and off for about twenty seconds while we walked down the stairs.

Later that evening, Mindy opened up her family scrapbook that was on the table in the living room. She showed everyone photos of her life in Asia and some childhood pictures of herself, growing up in Mississippi. She turned over one of the plastic-covered pages to a picture that I couldn't take my eyes off of. I knew immediately that it was of the same woman I had seen sitting on the couch in the sitting room.

"Who's the woman in that photo?" I asked, pointing to it.

"That's Mama. She died when I was seventeen. Not a day goes by that I don't think about her," Mindy said, speaking slowly.

"She looks like that Greek opera star...I can't remember the name," I said.

"Maria Callas! Yes, she does. She was also Greek," Mindy said.

I decided to wait to share what had happened to me. I didn't want to create any disturbance at the party.

About a week later, I told Mindy that I had seen her mother sitting on the sofa in the sitting room. She told me the sad story of losing her mother when she was still in high school. I reassured her how much her mother loves her and that she's still with her all the time.

Mindy's mother did not communicate with me that evening—she had seemed to want only to be part of the dinner party. The fact that she showed herself was evidence enough of her love for everyone.

Weeks later, I agreed to receive a personal reading from a medium who wanted to practice her mediumship skills. She lived 3000 miles away in Baja, Mexico. She knew very little about me, other than that I was a medium and would be able to provide reliable feedback to her after the practice reading. About halfway through the reading, she stopped to ask an unrelated question.

"Who's the woman you know who looks a lot like Maria Callas? This would be a woman that recently crossed your path," she asked. I was silent. *Is this medium in Mexico talking about what I think she's talking about?* I wondered.

"This woman in spirit says she was in the house with you...you don't remember?" she continued.

"Oh my God," I said. "Yes, I was in the house with a woman spirit who looks like Maria Callas. It was my friend Mindy's mother."

"Well, Mindy's mother wants everyone to know that she's still watching over her family," the Mexican medium said.

Mindy's deceased mother had appeared to me in Connecticut and was now making herself known to another medium—in *Mexico*. This was the first time anything like this had happened to me. Mindy's mother was making sure that her only daughter knew she was being watched over from the spirit world.

Later, when I told Mindy the rest of the story, it firmly reinforced her feeling that her mom was with her.

38

A Call from Heaven

"There's no use in trying. One can't believe impossible things."

—Alice, in *Alice in Wonderland*

For two days, my sister's potential memorial date was a heavy topic of discussion in my family. We couldn't agree on a date. Friends and family would be flying in from six different states. Attempting to please everyone—we all know how that goes. Lenore had lived up in the hills of Northwest Connecticut near the New York State line where the winters are long. The skiing is great, but travel can be treacherous. Because Lenore had been cremated, we were finally able to agree to wait a couple of months until the threat of snowstorms had passed.

On the Sunday night after Lenore had passed, I was watching the evening news when the phone rang.

"Jim, this is Sharon. Can I call you back in a few minutes?" Sharon asked.

Sharon was a medium and a member of our Circle of mediums who met twice a month. Her voice carried a tone of urgency.

"Sure. Where are you?" I asked. *Why would someone call, only to ask if they could call back?* I didn't ask her.

"I'm at church," Sharon said. She had never called me at home. I waited anxiously for her to call back. I hoped that everything was all right. Minutes later, the phone rang.

"Jim, the pastor of my church held a séance tonight. I need to tell you what happened," Sharon said hurriedly.

I knew that Sharon attended a local Spiritualist Church where the pastor was a psychic medium channel. He was able to channel the voices of spiritual beings and deliver messages to members of his congregation. The channeled spirit knew exactly what was going on in their daily lives and what questions they expected to hear answers for that particular evening. His channeled messages covered a wide range of topics from when a house would sell to astounding detailed information that included names, dates, and illnesses of deceased loved ones—all of this remarkable information brought forth without the church members asking a thing.

"Jim, I received a channeled message from the pastor tonight—he told me I'd probably leave Florida and move to North Carolina," Sharon said.

"Really? You were born and raised in Florida. You're not uprooting at this point in your life, are you?"

"Jim, I have a trip planned to North Carolina next month. I've considered making the move. I just hadn't told anyone yet," Sharon continued.

"I'd really miss you being a part of our Circle," I offered.

"Thanks Jim, but that's not why I called. The channel mentioned you by name. He had a personal message for you. He wanted me to call you. I'm still here at the church."

I became a bit frightened. I did not know the pastor, so the fact that my name came up got my attention. I didn't want to hear any bad news. What was so important that Sharon couldn't wait until she got home from church to call me?

"The channel asked me if I had a friend named James. He said to tell James that his sister Lenore recently arrived on the other side. He said she is fine and with her husband, Pat," Sharon said.

"What! Are you kidding me?" I shouted. I took a deep breath, then my critical mind took over. I was speechless. Question after question shot through my head. How on Earth could anyone in Florida have known that Lenore had died only two days earlier? How did he know her name? For that matter, how did he know her husband's name? And how did he know that her husband also had passed away? How did he *know my* name?

"There's more," Sharon whispered.

"My God. What else could there be?" I asked.

"He said that because of your sensitivities, Lenore will show herself to you," Sharon said.

My eyes filled with tears, and I prayed.

Epilogue

I wrote much of this memoir in 2010, but quickly put it away, believing that no one would be interested in my life experiences. I was also reluctant to share personal details that I considered to be an integral part of my spiritual development. Not to mention, I was, and continue to be, a medium still partially in the closet. I worried constantly that in being open about my ability, I'd ruin my professional reputation and become alienated from friends and family. I've seen this occur in the lives of other mediums.

Today, in 2023, I've embraced the fact that I'm a medium. I'm hopeful that reading about my experiences might help others who are trying to make sense of similar phenomenon. The world of mediumship has gained much international attention since I began training in 2008. A well-known international British medium recently stated that "mediumship has become a cottage industry."

My motivation to release this book at this time was two-fold. First, I am told that 85% of all mediums are female. *NO! NO! NO!* I thought when I heard this statistic. *The males must be hiding...like I was!* I hope my words might help other men to understand that they are not alone. The sensitivity necessary for this work has been bestowed upon all people, regardless of their gender.

Second, I am hopeful that readers might come to understand, if they have not already, that the work of the medium is spiritual in nature, and to treat it as such. Often the spiritual aspect can become sidetracked amidst a myriad of religious debate and ego involvement.

The foundation of our work is spiritual—when a medium sees the apparition of a deceased holy person, it is of course a spiritual event—and just as importantly, when the medium sees the apparition of a deceased relative, that too is spiritual work and should never be viewed as anything less. I view embracing my ability as a small step within my spiritual development. I pray often. Prior to accepting my ability, I did not pray regularly. I never understood its importance. Today, I am convinced that the words of prayer contain a special energy that has the ability to provide healing.

Today, I spend much less time questioning what this mystical phenomenon means or why clairvoyance and mediumship "happened to me." I accept that I will receive those answers when I reach the other side of the veil of human existence. Hopefully, society will come to an understanding and acceptance regarding these abilities. Science and love together are the integral components of the acceptance and understanding of life after death.

I am a clairvoyant, who, like my mother, was born with an ability to see those who have passed from this world. As I have shared, my communication with the other side came much later in my life. It was not *my* intention to become a psychic medium; it was God's intention.

A Final Note: Sharon did move to North Carolina, and my sister continues to be a huge help with my mediumship. And, in a few weeks I will be with my mother, celebrating her 100th birthday.

"When the mind soars in pursuit of things conceived in space, it pursues emptiness; but when man dives deep within himself, he experiences the fullness of existence."

—Meher Baba, 1977

Acknowledgments

By now, my decade-long reluctance to publish this book should be abundantly clear. Given that, my need to acknowledge those who stood by me with their encouragement is great.

I would be remiss not to thank Carole Lynne, the medium who first helped me to understand when I was opening to spirit.

Soon thereafter, my appreciation was boundless to have been connected with wonderful mediums I learned so much from during Circle: Sirry, Ron, Chris, Sharon, Karen, Kim, Carolyn, Mike, Michele and Tammie.

Years later there was Leona, Siobhan, and Stacey who continue to this day to inspire me with their teaching and knowledge.

Very special thanks to Michelle Robin, whose ability to share, discuss, entertain, and enlighten always amazes me ... and not to mention encourage our regular visits to the Arthur Findlay College of Psychic Science in Great Britain.

Prayers are sent to my sister Lenore in spirit. Before she passed, she promised to help me with my mediumship from the other side. She has kept her word.

Love to my 100-year-old mother who saw spirits throughout many lonely years when there was no one to talk to about her experience.

I was blessed to have been able to work with a caring and creative publisher and editor duo, Penelope Love and Jaime Cox. Their expertise was combined with an acceptance and understanding of the metaphysical world.

A million thanks for my writing instructor, Julie Gilbert, who somehow was able to convince me that I could write this book by myself without a ghostwriter.

Finally, love to my wife, Sallie, who never failed to support me. She was understanding throughout the years when neither of us totally understood what was happening. Now we do!

Publisher's Note

Thank you for the opportunity to serve you. If you would like to help share this message, here are some popular ways:

REVIEWS
Write an online review and tag #thebirthofanamericanmedium and #jamesdeary

GIVING
Gift the print or audiobook to friends, family and colleagues

BOOK CLUBS
Request a Reading Group Guide and an author visit: Info@CitrinePublishing.com

WORKSHOPS & SPEAKING
Invite James Deary to speak with your organization or organize a workshop: Info@CitrinePublishing.com

BULK ORDERS
+1-828-585-7030 or Sales@CitrinePublishing.com

We appreciate your book reviews, letters, and shares.

Citrine Publishing